Media Images and Representations

CONTEMPORARY NATIVE AMERICAN ISSUES

Economic Issues and Development

Education and Language Restoration

Media Images and Representations

Political Issues

Sacred Sites and Repatriation

Social Life and Issues

Media Images and Representations

C. Richard King
Associate Professor of Comparative Ethnic Studies,
Washington State University

Foreword by
Walter Echo-Hawk
Senior Staff Attorney, Native American Rights Fund

Introduction by
Paul Rosier
Assistant Professor of History, Villanova University

CHELSEA HOUSE
PUBLISHERS
A Haights Cross Communications Company ®

Philadelphia

CHELSEA HOUSE PUBLISHERS

VP, New Product Development Sally Cheney
Director of Production Kim Shinners
Creative Manager Takeshi Takahashi
Manufacturing Manager Diann Grasse

Staff for MEDIA IMAGES AND REPRESENTATIONS

Executive Editor Lee Marcott
Editor Christian Green
Production Editor Bonnie Cohen
Photo Editor Sarah Bloom
Series and Cover Designer Takeshi Takahashi
Layout EJB Publishing Services

©2006 by Chelsea House Publishers,
a subsidiary of Haights Cross Communications.

A Haights Cross Communications ✈ Company ®

www.chelseahouse.com

First Printing

9 8 7 6 5 4 3 2 1

Library of Congress Cataloging-in-Publication Data

King, C. Richard, 1968-
  Media images and representations / C. Richard King.
    p. cm. — (Contemporary Native American issues)
  Includes bibliographical references and index.
  ISBN 0-7910-7968-6 (hard cover)
  1. Indians in mass media. I. Title. II. Series.
  P94.5.I53K56 2005
  791.43'653997—dc22
                                    2005007546

All links and web addresses were checked and verified to be correct at the time of publication.
Because of the dynamic nature of the web, some addresses and links may have changed since
publication and may no longer be valid.

Contents

Foreword by Walter Echo-Hawk   vi

Introduction by Paul Rosier   xi

1 Introduction and Overview   1

2 Films and Television   10

3 Journalistic Coverage   31

4 Mascots   52

5 Indigenous Media   71

6 The Internet and the Future
   of Native Americans in the Media   89

   Chronology   104

   Notes   105

   Bibliography   108

   Further Reading/Websites   110

   Index   111

Foreword

Walter Echo-Hawk

Native Americans share common aspirations, and a history and fate with indigenous people around the world. International law defines indigenous peoples as non-European populations who resided in lands colonized by Europeans before the colonists arrived. The United Nations estimates that approximately 300 million persons worldwide are variously known as tribal, Native, aboriginal, or indigenous. From 1492 to 1945, European nations competed to conquer, colonize, and Christianize the rest of the world. Indigenous peoples faced a difficult, life-altering experience, because colonization invariably meant the invasion of their homelands, appropriation of their lands, destruction of their habitats and ways of life, and sometimes genocide.

Though colonialism was repudiated and most colonies achieved independence, the circumstances of indigenous peoples has not improved in countries where newly independent nations adopted the preexisting colonial system for dealing with indigenous peoples. In such nations, colonial patterns still exist. The paramount challenge to human rights in these nations, including our own, is to find just ways to protect the human, political, cultural, and property rights of their indigenous people.

Contemporary issues, including those of culture, can be understood against the backdrop of colonialism and the closely related need to strengthen laws to protect indigenous rights. For example, colonists invariably retained close cultural ties to their distant homelands and rarely adopted their indigenous neighbors' values, cultures, or ways of looking at Mother Earth. Instead, they imposed their cultures, languages, and religions upon tribal people through the use of missionaries, schools, soldiers, and governments.

In the mid-1800s, U.S. government policymakers used the "Vanishing Red Man" theory, which was advanced by anthropologists at the time, as justification for the forcible removal of Native American tribes and for taking their lands. The policy did not work; America's indigenous peoples did not "vanish" as predicted. Native American tribes are still here despite suffering great difficulties since the arrival of Europeans, including an enormous loss of life and land brought on by disease, warfare, and genocide. Nonetheless, diverse groups survived, thrived, and continue to be an important part of American society.

Today, Native Americans depend on domestic law to protect their remaining cultural integrity but often that law is weak and ill-suited for the task, and sometimes does not exist at all. For example, U.S. federal law fails to protect indigenous holy places, even though other nations throughout the world take on the responsibility of protecting sacred sites within their borders. Congress is aware of this loophole in religious liberty but does not remedy it. Other laws promote assimilation, like the "English only" laws that infringe upon the right of Native Americans to retain their indigenous languages.

Another example concerns indigenous property rights. The *very* purpose of colonialism was to provide riches, property, and resources for European coffers. To that end, a massive one-way transfer of property from indigenous to nonindigenous hands occurred in most colonies. This included land, natural resources, and personal property (called *artifacts* by anthropologists). Even dead bodies (called *specimens* or *archaeological resources* by anthropologists) were dug up and carried away. The appropriation has been extended to intellectual property: aboriginal plant and animal knowledge patented by corporations; tribal names, art, and symbols converted into trademarks; and religious beliefs and practices *borrowed* by members of the New Age movement. Even tribal identities have been taken by "wannabes" masquerading as Native Americans for personal, professional, or commercial gain. In beleaguered Native eyes, little else is left to take. Native legal efforts attempt to stem and reverse this one-way transfer of property and protect what little remains.

Through it all, Native American tribes have played an important role in the American political system. The U.S. Constitution describes the political relationships among the federal government, states, Native American tribes, and foreign nations. Hundreds of tribal governments comprise our political system as "domestic dependent nations." They exercise power over Native American reservations, provide for their tribal citizens, engage in economic development, and sometimes come into conflict with states over intergovernmental disputes. Many tribes own and manage vast tracts of tribal land, extensive water rights, and other natural resources. The United States holds legal title to this property in trust. As trustee, the United States exercises significant power over the lives of Native Americans and their communities; and it is responsible for their well-being. These "nations within nations" are not found on international maps and are invisible to many in our own country.

Prior to 1900, about five hundred treaties between Native American tribes and the United States were duly ratified by the Senate and signed into law by the president. Treaties contain hard-fought agreements that were earned on American battlefields and made between Native American tribes and the United States. They opened vast expanses of Native American land to white settlement, protected remaining Native property, and created the political relationships with the U.S. government that remain to this day. As President George H.W. Bush said during his inaugural address in 1989, "great nations like great men must keep their word." Though many treaties were broken, many promises are honored by the United States today and upheld by federal courts.

The history, heritage, and aspirations of Native Americans create many challenges today. Concern for tribal sovereignty, self-determination, and cultural survival are familiar among Native Americans. Their struggles to protect treaty rights (such as hunting, fishing, and gathering rights), achieve freedom of religion, and protect Mother Earth (including land, resources, and habitat) are commonplace challenges, and sometimes include the task of repatriating dead relatives from museums. Each year, Congress passes laws affecting vital Native interests and the Supreme Court decides crucial cases. The hardships that Native Americans have endured to keep their identity are little known to many Americans. From the times of Red Cloud, Seattle, and Chief Joseph, Native leaders have fought to achieve these freedoms for their people. These ideals even today motivate many Native American soldiers to fight for our country in distant lands, like Iraq and Afghanistan, with the hope that the principles fought for abroad will be granted to their relatives at home.

Today, vibrant Native American communities make significant contributions to our rich national heritage. Evidence of this can be found in the recently opened National Museum of the American Indian, in Washington, D.C. It is also found throughout the pages of *Native Peoples* magazine and other Native media. It fills the best galleries, museums, and auction houses. It can be seen in the art, dance, music, philosophy, religion, literature, and film made by Native Americans, which rank among the world's finest. Visitors crowd tribal casinos and other enterprises that dot Native American reservations in growing numbers. Tribal governments, courts, and agencies are more sophisticated than ever before. Native American-controlled schools and colleges are restoring the importance of culture, traditions, and elders in education, and instill Native pride in students. The determination to retain indigenous cultures can be seen through the resurgence of tribal language, culture, and religious ceremonial life.

Yet many old problems persist. Too many Native Americans are impoverished and in poor health; living at the very bottom of almost all socioeconomic indicators and often in violence-ridden communities where disease, such as AIDS, knows no racial or cultural boundaries. Some socioeconomic problems stem from the aftermath of colonization of Native lands, peoples, and resources, or from efforts to stamp out Native culture and religion. Others stem from prejudice and hostility against Native people that has long characterized race relations in the United States.

As our nation matures, we must reject, once and for all, harmful policies and notions of assimilation and ethnocentrism, and embrace cultural relativism in our relations with the Native peoples who comprise our diverse society. History teaches where racial stereotypes, myths, and fictions prevail, human rights violations soon follow. But social change comes slowly and ethnocentrism remains deeply rooted in mass media and other corners of society. To little avail, Native people have told Hollywood to stop stereotyping Native Americans, protested against harmful racial stereotypes used by groups like the "Redskin" football team, and requested appropriate coverage of Native issues by the mainstream media. Native life is far different than how it has been depicted in the movies and by school and professional mascots.

Regrettably, schools do not teach us about Native Americans; textbooks largely ignore the subject. Sidebar information is provided only when Pilgrims or other American heroes are discussed, but Native Americans mostly "disappear" after dining with Pilgrims, leaving students to wonder about their fate. As a result, the people who met Columbus, Coronado, Custer, and Lewis and Clark are still here, but remain a mystery to legislators, policymakers, and judges who decide vital Native interests. Those interests are too often overlooked, marginalized, or subordinated by the rest of society. The widespread lack of education and information is the most serious problem confronting America's Native people today.

CONTEMPORARY NATIVE AMERICAN ISSUES will help remedy the information gap and enable youth to better understand the issues mentioned above. We are fortunate to have comprehensive data compiled in this series for students. Armed with facts, this generation can address Native American challenges justly.

Walter R. Echo-Hawk
Boulder, Colorado
March 2005

Introduction

Paul Rosier

During the mid-1970s, I attended Swarthmore High School in suburban Philadelphia, Pennsylvania. There, I learned little about Native Americans other than that they had lived in teepees, hunted buffalo, and faced great hardships in adapting to modern life at the end of the nineteenth century. But I learned nothing about Native Americans' experiences in the twentieth century. And as a member of the Tomahawks, the high school football team, I was constantly reminded that Native Americans had been violent and had used primitive weapons like tomahawks. Movies and television shows reinforced these notions in my young and impressionable mind.

It is my experience from teaching Native American history at the university level that students in middle and high schools across the country, have not, with some exceptions, learned much more about Native Americans in the twentieth century than I did thirty years ago. Several years ago, one of my students asked me if Native Americans still live in tepees. He and many others like him continue to be presented with a limited and biased interpretation of Native Americans, largely from popular culture, especially sports, where professional teams, such as the Washington Redskins, and mascots, such as the University of Illinois' Chief Illiniwek, continue to portray Native Americans as historical objects, not as citizens of this nation and as members of distinct tribal communities.

In 1990, President George H.W. Bush approved a joint resolution of Congress that designated November National Indian Heritage Month, and over the following years similar proclamations were made by presidents William J. Clinton and George W. Bush. On November 1, 1997, President Clinton stated: "As we enter the next millennium we have an exciting opportunity to open a new era of understanding, cooperation, and respect among all of America's people. We must work together to tear down the walls of separation and mistrust and build a strong foundation for the future." In November 2001, President Bush echoed Clinton by saying, "I call on all Americans to learn more about the history and heritage of the Native peoples of this great land. Such actions reaffirm our appreciation and respect for their traditions and way of life and can help to preserve an important part of our culture for generations yet to come."

We still have work to do to further "understanding, cooperation, and respect among all of America's people" and to "learn more about the history and heritage of the Native peoples of this great land." The information presented in CONTEMPORARY NATIVE AMERICAN ISSUES is designed to address the challenges set forth by presidents Clinton and Bush, and debunk the inaccurate perceptions of Native Americans that stretches back to our nation's founding and continues today. For example, schoolchildren's first intellectual exposure to Native Americans may well be through the Declaration of Independence, which describes Native Americans as "merciless Indian savages, whose known rule of warfare is an undistinguished destruction of all ages, sexes, and conditions."

The series' authors are scholars who have studied and written about the issues that affect today's Native Americans. Each scholar committed to write for this series because they share my belief that educating our youth about Native Americans should begin earlier in our schools and that the subject matter should be presented accurately.

Outside the classroom, young students' first visual exposure to Native Americans likely comes from sporting contests or in popular culture. First impressions matter. C. Richard King, Associate Professor of Comparative Ethnic Studies at Washington State University, discusses this important issue in his volume, *Media Images and Representations.* King looks at how these early impressions of Native Americans persist in film and television, journalism, sports mascots, indigenous media, and the internet. But he also looks at how Native Americans themselves have protested these images and tried to create new ones that more accurately reflect their history, heritage, and contemporary attitudes.

In *Education and Language Restoration,* Jon Allan Reyhner examines the history of how Native Americans have been educated in boarding schools or mission schools to become assimilated into mainstream American society. Reyhner, Professor of Education at Northern Arizona University, considers how Native Americans have recently created educational systems to give students the opportunity to learn about their culture and to revitalize dormant languages. Like non-Native American students, Native students should invest time and energy in learning about Native American culture and history.

This educational process is important to help Native Americans deal with a myriad of social problems that affects many communities in our country. In their volume *Social Life and Issues,* Roe W. Bubar and Irene S. Vernon, professors at the Center for Applied Studies in American Ethnicity at Colorado State University, review the various social issues that Native Americans face, including health problems like AIDS and alcoholism. They also consider how Native American communities try to resolve these social and health crises by using traditional healing ceremonies and religious practices that are hundreds of years old.

One very important issue that has helped Native American communities heal is repatriation. Joe Edward Watkins, Associate Professor of Anthropology at the University of New Mexico, examines this significant matter in his volume, *Sacred Sites and Repatriation.* Repatriation involves the process of the government returning to individual tribes the remains of ancestors stolen from graves in the nineteenth century, as well as pots and ceremonial objects also taken from graves or stolen from reservations. Native Americans have fought for the return of objects and remains but also to protect sacred sites from being developed. Such places have religious or spiritual meaning and their protection is important to ensure continued practice of traditional ceremonies that allow Native Americans to address the social and health problems that Vernon and Bubar describe.

In *Political Issues*, Deborah Welch, the Director of the Public History Program and Associate Professor of History at Longwood University, writes about how Native Americans reclaimed political power and used it to strengthen their communities through legislation that promoted both repatriation and the protection of sacred sites, as well as their ability to practice their religion and traditions, which the federal government had prohibited into the 1970s. Native American tribal communities have fought for their sovereignty for decades. Sovereignty means that tribal governments set the rules and regulations for living within reservation boundaries. Federally recognized tribal groups maintain their own courts to prosecute crimes—with the exception of major crimes, that is, rape, arson, and murder. Native Americans living on their own reservations generally do not need to obey state regulations pertaining to hunting and fishing and do not pay state income or excise taxes, though they are responsible for paying federal income taxes.

Tribal governments also help to create economic opportunities for their people, the subject of Deborah Welch's second volume, *Economic Issues and Development*. In this book, Welch examines the ways in which Native Americans have tried to create employment in businesses, which include ranching, mining, golf resorts, and casinos. She also considers how Native Americans have tried to develop projects within the context of their environmental traditions. As with other elements of their lives, Native Americans try to use their tribal histories and ceremonies to confront the economic challenges of modern life; to prosper by being *both* Native and American, while ensuring the health of Mother Earth.

Limited coverage of Native American life in schools, newspapers, and broadcast media has helped to perpetuate Americans' stereotypical views of Native Americans as either wealthy from gambling or suffering from poverty and alcoholism. The real picture is not so easy to paint and involves more than 560 separate Native American nations within the United States, which includes 4.1 million people who identify themselves as solely or in part Native American. The goal of this series is to explore the many different dimensions of the complex world of today's Native Americans, who are divided by geography, politics, traditions, goals, and even by what they want to be called, Native American or American Indian. Most Native Americans, however, prefer to be identified by their tribal name, for example, Lakota (Sioux), Blackfeet, or Diné (Navajo). And yet Native Americans are some of the most patriotic Americans, in part because their ancestors and relatives have died fighting in the name of freedom, a freedom that has allowed them to be both Native and American. As U.S. Army Sergeant Leonard Gouge of the Oklahoma Muscogee Creek community put it shortly after the September 11 attacks, "By supporting the American way of life, I am preserving the Indian way of life."

Paul Rosier
Villanova, Pennsylvania
March 2005

1

Introduction and Overview

Arriving early at my dentist's office, I rummaged through the magazines in the waiting area. Happily, amid the glossy entertainment weeklies and the news periodicals, I found an August 18, 2003 issue of *Sports Illustrated*. Although Bill Parcells, new coach of the Dallas Cowboys, glared out at me from the cover, what caught my eye was a piece on Jordin Tootoo, who at the time was poised to be the first Inuk to play in the National Hockey League as a member of the Nashville Predators.[1] Pleased to see a story on an indigenous athlete in a major periodical, I quickly turned to "On the Wild Side," reading it both as a sports fan and as a scholar who teaches and writes about Native Americans in popular culture. I delighted in the profile of the emerging superstar, which recorded an array of disparate facts about his youth, his indigenous community in northern Canada, his family, his abilities, his hobbies, and his aspirations. On the other hand, I was troubled over the words and metaphors used to paint a portrait of Tootoo, unsure how readers might interpret them.

The article presented the racial heritage of the Inuk athlete in a way that would never be allowed in a story on a white athlete. Comparing Tootoo's appearance with that of his father, the author notes, "A full-blooded Inuk, Barney's skin is the color of saddle leather, darker than Jordin's. Father and son are broad-chested and short, with bright, dark eyes and high cheekbones" (Barney's wife, Rose, is of Ukrainian descent.)[2]

Similarly, the metaphors employed to describe Tootoo are eery echoes of images of Native American individuals and institutions viewed as savage throughout history. In fact, throughout the article, the central image of the hockey player is that of the predator. The article begins with a lengthy account of a hunt, noting, "wearing yellow slicker pants smeared with bloodstains . . . rifle in hand, he looks every bit the predator—or is it Predator."[3] Later, it details how Tootoo eats raw meat and fish and was cast in the role of an enforcer on the ice. The portrait of Tootoo, I fear, suggests that indigenous people really are violent, natural, and savage.

When describing Tootoo's social world, the article is little better. It repeatedly notes the isolation of his home community, Rankin Inlet, and its proximity to the Arctic Circle. It contrasts the recent past in which the seminomadic Inuk hunted seal and caribou and ate their prey uncooked with the settled life of today, featuring electricity, single-family homes, and a fully stocked grocery. It speaks in near surprise about the presence of a pizza shop, satellite television, Internet access, and all-terrain vehicles among people who still practice traditional ways. Although change is obvious, the way it is presented in the feature on Tootoo reinforces generally accepted, and entirely false, notions that indigenous peoples are unsophisticated and technologically backward, in short, primitive.

The story on Jordin Tootoo deserves so much attention not because it is unusual, but rather because it illustrates many of

Jordin Tootoo, a right winger on the Nashville Predators, became the first Inuk to play hockey in the National Hockey League, when he made his debut in 2003. Unfortunately, Native people such as Tootoo are sometimes stereotyped by the mainstream media, who often paint false and hurtful portraits of them.

the predominant relationships between American Indians and the mass media in the United States over the past century. Consequently, it reveals the central themes of this book.

Perhaps most obviously, it attests to the continuing vitality of stereotypes. A stereotype is a representation of a group of people that reduces them to a set of essential characteristics. Such simplified and false images tend to be accepted as natural facts and rank people through assessments of their capacities, character, or culture. Stereotypes about racial and ethnic groups have proven powerful and persistent. They need not have malicious intent, nor be derisive, as in the idea that all Indians are drunks. Frequently, racial stereotypes are complex statements that give voice to accepted understandings about what it means to live a good life, be human, be smart, be a decent person, and so on. They color and misconstrue the world around us, valuing other bodies, beliefs, and behaviors for how well they correspond to the norms of Euro-American society. The story about Jordin Tootoo, for instance, bundles together references to the location of Rankin Inlet, technological change, goods for sale at the market, and businesses in the community to make it comprehensible to readers. In the process, it stresses simple, fundamental differences that collapse the complexities of Inuk life to a set of surprising, amusing, and clichéd features that distinguish it from everyday life in the supposedly civilized world inhabited by the readers of *Sports Illustrated*. And Tootoo is not merely a young man who enjoys hunting with his father. Instead, he is rendered as a predator, a natural hunter, who possesses unstated attributes, if not inherent skills, and who seemingly needs to kill to survive.

Stereotyping, as the *Sports Illustrated* feature on Tootoo suggests, is at the heart of how the mainstream media relates to and represents indigenous peoples. In many ways, this is nothing new. It reflects the long history of distortion, misunderstanding, and racism that has characterized Euro-American images of and interactions with Native Americans. Modern visions of Indians derive from early Christian attributions of sin and savagery to the beliefs and behaviors of American Indians; romantic celebrations of Native peoples as noble children of nature; debates around federal policies directed at removal and assimilation paired with ongoing wars designed to subdue and subjugate Native nations; and scientific racism intent to assess and rank American Indians based on cranial capacity, material culture, and ways of reckoning kinship. With the emergence of mass culture at the end of the nineteenth century, these disparate sources came together, informing the representations of indigenous peoples in the stories told about in dime novels and in the wildly popular dramas staged as a part of Wild West shows. These new cultural forms wove together ideas and assumptions that would become central to media accounts of Native Americans, notably a cast of characters (the warrior, the noble savage, the loyal sidekick, the chief, the princess, and the squaw) and a set of stories (the settling of the frontier, unprovoked transgressions by hostiles, the inevitable and tragic disappearance of once-proud peoples, intercultural conflict, and Euro-American treachery). Over the course of the twentieth and into the twenty-first century, cinema, television, journalism, and sports would rely on and endlessly recycle these figures and fables to entertain audiences, offer interpretations of American history, and pay tribute to Native Americans.

Stereotypes have flourished in the media precisely because of the organization of the media in the United States. In a society centered upon and dominated by Euro-Americans, when thinking about Native Americans and the media, it is crucial to ask: What sort of stories and images circulate? Who authors these stories and creates these images? Why? Who owns the means of mass communication? Today, as in the past, Euro-Americans (as authors, editors, directors, producers, and actors) craft most media accounts of indigenous peoples. This is as true of the *Sports Illustrated* story on Jordin Tootoo as it is of *Dances with Wolves*, the celebrated film directed by Kevin Costner that centers on a white army officer who goes Native in the nineteenth century. Moreover, the questions asked and the interpretations of the answers given in turn tend to come from outside Native communities, reflecting the preoccupations and values of mainstream society. Finally, media ownership is concentrated in Euro-American hands.

Stereotypes and structures have long silenced indigenous

peoples. On the one hand, the media have substituted false images of Indians for accurate accounts of the history, diversity, and vitality of Native America. On the other hand, only rarely have they created a space in which indigenous peoples could speak for themselves, about themselves, and about their concerns. This pattern of silencing has meant that most Americans have limited understandings of Indian life and almost no familiarity with indigenous perspectives.

Not surprisingly, most of readers of *Sports Illustrated*, in common with the majority of Americans, surely were unaware that 2003 not only marked the professional debut of Jordin Tootoo in the NHL but also was the 175th anniversary of the *Cherokee Phoenix*, the first newspaper published in a Native American language. If indigenous involvement in the media has remained hidden, masked by popular images and inhibited by social barriers, its presence is ever more important. For at least a century, Native Americans have challenged media images, criticizing them for misrepresenting their lives and cultures, while calling attention to their negative effects. At the same time, American Indians increasingly have taken an active role in media production as writers, directors, actors, and owners. Together, activism and involvement promise to reshape the future relationships between Native Americans and the media.

In spite of these developments, many would argue that mass media are trivial, little more than frivolous distractions that grant their audiences moments of pleasure and escapes from everyday life. Nothing could be further from the truth. Native Americans comprise a small fraction of the population, and many Americans rarely, if ever, have face-to-face interactions with them. Indeed, films, television, the Internet, journalism, and even sports mascots provide the central means through which Americans encounter and formulate interpretations of indigenous peoples. Consequently, while the mainstream media may in fact use Indians and popular understandings of them to tell amusing and engaging stories,

Chief Wahoo, the Cleveland Indians' mascot, has represented the Major League Baseball team since 1915. The Cleveland mascot typifies the way Native Americans have been portrayed over the last century—more as cartoon-like characters with red skin, buck teeth, and often donning a headdress or feather.

create playful and fun diversions, and convey profound statements about the human condition, at the same time, they encourage audiences to think about themselves and the world around them: they shape how Americans think about themselves and their history; they paint false and hurtful portraits of indigenous people, casting them as subordinate, invisible, inhuman; they perpetuate anti-Indian racism; and they influence social policy. Not surprisingly, the media constitute a key space in which Native Americans have sought to reclaim control over the stories told about them, correct false images, and create new ways of understanding Native Americans.

The five chapters that follow endeavor to offer a fairly comprehensive overview of the relationships between Native

Americans and the media. Individually, they examine film and television, journalism, sports mascots, indigenous media, and the Internet, weaving together a century-long history of misinterpretation. And while a significant portion of the text will be devoted to continuity and change within the image of Native Americans in the media, throughout, attention will be directed at the increasingly important role of Indians as actors, directors, creative artists, reporters, critics, and consumers. Because films and television have proven pivotal to popular conceptions of indigenous people, the study begins with these genres. In particular, it analyzes the shifting stereotypes through which these media imagined Indians and recent efforts to reimagine them. Against this backdrop, the third chapter examines Native Americans and the press. As in the second chapter, much of the discussion here centers on issues of imagery and interpretation. Despite claims of objectivity, journalistic coverage, in common with films and television programming, has always been biased, often with disastrous consequences for Native communities. Building on these discussions of stereotyping, the fourth chapter turns to sports mascots, revealing both the persistence of anti-Indian racism and the possibility for change when indigenous peoples and their allies work to counter injurious imagery. Reading the newspaper, watching an old western, or cheering on the home team, most would never guess that for more than 150 years, Native Americans have actively participated in media production. Looking at indigenous media, the fifth chapter offers an overview of the history and significance of this participation. The final chapter discusses Indians in cyberspace. It is particularly concerned with the ways this new medium reinforces and revolutionizes historic relationships, outlining its implications for the future of indigenous people in mass communications and American society more generally.

Before proceeding, a few words about terminology are in order. Throughout this text, the terms *Native American, Indian, American Indian, indigenous,* and *indigenous peoples* will be used interchangeably to refer to the many diverse ethnic and political groups who originally inhabited the area now referred to as North America. This choice reflects both common usage and ongoing struggles over the politics of naming ethnic groups in the contemporary United States. Many find "Native American" to be preferable, because it parallels terms employed for other racial groups—for instance, African American—and avoids Columbus' misrecognition of the inhabitants of the Western Hemisphere as East Indians. At the same time, many others refuse the label "Native American." Cultural conservatives often opine that all who were born in the United States are Native Americans. Moreover, many of those to whom the name refers find it awkward, hollow, and overly academic; they think of themselves as "Indian" or "American Indian" (or better, as members of a tribe) and use that to describe themselves and their peers. Complicating matters further, academics and activists have proffered the term *indigenous* as more desirable. With all of these complexities in mind, I employ all these terms, in part to underscore the politics of naming without policing language or thought. It is hoped that refusing a single name will make clear to the reader the complexities and diversities of living in and studying contemporary indigenous communities in North America.

2

Films and Television

In 1911, in an essay on "Moving Picture Absurdities," W. Stephen Bush reviewed Hollywood's pervasive image of the American Indian in film:

> The greatest of them all is the Indian. We have him in every variety but one. We have Indians a la Français, "red" men recruited from the Bowery and upper West End Avenue. We have Licensed Indians and Independent Indians—the only kind we lack are the real Indians . . . He is either wholly good, seemingly transplanted from the skies, or else a fiend and an expert scalper in constant practice . . . You cannot escape the moving picture Indian. Recently, I visited five moving picture houses in a Southern tour and five in a city in New England. The Indian was everywhere.[4]

The same year, a group of Native Americans gathered in Washington, D.C., to protest cinematic representations. An article in

Moving Picture World summarized the grievances expressed about one recent release in which

> a young Indian graduate of one of the non-reservation schools was the chief figure. He was shunned by the members of his tribe upon his return to them, took to drink, killed a man and fled, but was killed after a long chase. This was denounced as an untrue portrayal of the Indians.[5]

These two early snapshots underscore two of the central themes of this chapter: American Indians have been ubiquitous in American cinema and almost without exception representations of them in movies and television have been false. Indeed, as many scholars and critics have suggested ever since Bush, on the screen, audiences do not encounter real Indians, but meet the Hollywood Indian, a fictional, stereotypical, and profitable rendering that says more about Euro-American presuppositions and preoccupations than it does about indigenous peoples.

This chapter addresses the history and significance of the Hollywood Indian. Specifically, it analyzes the stereotypes and stories through which movies and television have represented Native American cultures and histories, and more importantly, why such inaccurate and hurtful images persist. Following a history of Indians in film, the discussion reviews the major themes and trends of cinematic and televisual representations of indigenous peoples of North America.

BEFORE FILM

To fully appreciate the depiction of American Indians, as well as the portrayal of relations with Euro-Americans and mainstream society, it is necessary to review Wild West shows. For nearly a half century, Wild West shows combined historical re-enactment, melodrama, elements of indigenous cultures, and proto-rodeo forms, offering interpretations of the American west, Indian/white relations, and American history. From their beginnings in 1883 through their disappearance in the early 1930s, these entertainments both reflected and extended prevailing understandings of the frontier and American Indians.

Wild West Shows

Wild West shows staged renowned battles, including the Battle of the Little Bighorn, western conflicts like the attack on the Deadwood Stage, and grand epic narratives, such as "The Drama of Civilization," adding Native American dance, cowboy bands, and athletic events (steer roping and bronco riding) to these more familiar dramatic forms. Wild West shows began to emerge at a pivotal moment in American history: at the end of military campaign against indigenous peoples. In this context, they encouraged Americans to grapple with questions of racial difference and cultural evolution, while prompting nostalgic yearnings for nature, tradition, and indigenous communities destroyed by progress and manifest destiny.

Wild West shows have had a profound impact on American culture. They cemented popular conceptions of the region, connecting it with guns, conflict, the frontier, and the cowboy. Wild West shows, moreover, set the terms in which many Americans would come to know Native Americans. This image stressed wildness and bellicosity, suggesting that indigenous peoples were best understood as historical artifacts, bypassed by progress. At the same time, they rendered Indian/white relations, underscoring not merely a violent clash of cultures, but the just conquest and subjugation of the Native nations of North America. In many respects, Wild West shows shaped the content of the film industry, influencing the characters and narratives of the western for much of the century.

THE EARLY YEARS OF AMERICAN CINEMA

Films featuring Native American themes date to the very beginnings of American cinema, proving to be a popular staple within the entertainment industry. Indeed, University of

Colorado professor Ward Churchill estimates that two thousand movies and ten thousand television episodes with Indian themes have been produced since the end of the nineteenth

Typecasting the Native Warrior

Many would agree that war dehumanizes soldiers and citizens alike. Less understood is the ways in which the language and images associated with war dehumanize as well.

Native Americans have long suffered stereotyping and other symbolic injuries when they have come into conflict with mainstream society. Cast as bellicose and savage, the indigenous warrior occupied the national imagination for more than a century. Newspapers delighted in recounting the terrifying acts of inhumanity perpetuated in raids and unprovoked attacks by American Indians. This ceaseless demonization of indigenous peoples served to justify the taking of lands from them and the waging of war against them. It also has rendered invisible the countless Native American patriots who have defended the United States in every conflict since the Revolutionary War.

Sadly, warfare continues to encourage misrepresentation of American Indians. Although often unrecognized, the ongoing war in Iraq reiterates many of these patterns. The popular notion of the Indian warrior has played a key role in the naming of weapons systems. Thus, U.S. forces fly Comanche helicopters into battle and launch tomahawk missiles at enemy positions. Commanders, unaware of the meaning of Thanksgiving to many indigenous peoples and unfamiliar with the devastating wars the Pilgrims waged against Native nations, did not give a second thought to dubbing a military action against Iraqi insurgents in November 2004, "Operation Mayflower."

And while the media fails to question such language and its effects, it has extended historic harms as well. Some commentators, following the lead of military commanders, have referred to Iraq and Afghanistan as Indian Country, suggesting that the conflict is best thought of on the model of Indian Wars of old, with heroic Americans facing hostile Natives. Such imagery, moreover, disrespects the patriotic Native soldiers fighting and dying for their country, including Lori Ann Piestewa (Hopi), whose sacrifice was all but eclipsed by the media frenzy over the rescue of her compatriot Jessica Lynch.

century.[6] In part, the centrality of American Indians to the entertainment industry, particularly in relation to Euro-American society, stems from the malleability of the imagined Indian that could be romanticized or demonized, pitied or pilloried, a figure open to reinterpretation by successive generations of white writers, directors, and audiences. Additionally, Native Americans have played such a fundamental role in movies and television, precisely because the conquest of the continent, and the associated displacement, dispossession, and ethnic violence have proven crucial to the formulation of American history and national identity.

American Indians made their cinematic debut in the 1890s. Perhaps their earliest and most famous appearance was in a series of short films, known as actualities, produced by Thomas Edison in 1894. Not surprisingly, these not only seized on the popularity of Buffalo Bill Cody and his Wild West show, but some actually featured the famed scout and entertainer, along with members of his troupe of performers. Others, including *Sioux Ghost Dance* and *Indian War Council*, sought to portray recent events. Four years later, Edison again returned to American Indian themes, shooting dances and daily life on location. While the content of these earliest films varied, they have two things in common: first they endeavored to be detailed and authentic portraits of Indian life; and, second, they presented Native Americans through established clichés, namely warriors adorned in "war paint and feathers . . . brandishing tomahawks and scalping knives," which undermined their ethnographic intentions.[7] The work done at Edison's New Jersey studio laid the foundation for subsequent work done in the silent film era.

During the first three decades of the twentieth century, as technology became more sophisticated and the industry more accepted, the popularity of Indian-themed films grew. In this period, actualities faded into history, as melodrama and military conflict increasingly dominated the silver screen.

In 1883, William Frederick Cody, also known as "Buffalo Bill," established his Wild West show, which was a reenactment of frontier life and dramatized some of the important historical events of the West. Cody's show, which included famed Hunkpapa Sioux chief Sitting Bull (shown here with Cody), ran for more than three decades and even toured Europe.

Importantly, in contrast with any era of film history before the present, Native Americans held prominent creative roles in the industry: James Young Deer (Winnebago) made *Yaqui Girl* and *White Fawn's Devotion* (1910) before serving in the military during WWI, Edwin Carewe (Cherokee) directed *Ramona* in

1928, and Molly Spotted Elk (Penobscot) starred in *Silent Enemy* in 1930. It would be decades before American Indians would attain prominence in the industry again. Of greater immediate and lasting significance, Wild West shows exerted a powerful influence, and not just through the stereotypes and storylines they had made famous. On the one hand, performers,

Forgotten Filmmakers

Before the studio system dominated Hollywood and the formulaic western ruled the popular imagination, American Indians played a more active role in the production of cinematic images. Unfortunately, these early artists have been all but forgotten. The careers of James Young Deer and Lillian St. Cyr (Princess Red Wing) tell us much about what was.

Young Deer, a former performer in Wild West shows and traveling circuses, began working as a writer and actor for Hollywood film companies Kalem and Lubin in the early years of the twentieth century. He met St. Cyr while the two starred in *Red Wing's Gratitude* in 1909. Married that same year, they moved from New Jersey to Los Angeles, where they established themselves as rising talents. Two years later, Young Deer was head of the Pathe company's West Coast studio. There, he and St. Cyr wrote, directed, and starred in a number of films, including *The Prospector and the Indian* and *Red Eagle, the Lawyer*.

Although over the course of their careers, Young Deer and St. Cyr increasingly played off prevailing expectations of Indians and Indianness, they worked ceaselessly to challenge popular stereotypes. In fact, in their films they sought to simultaneously validate Indianness, while critiquing white society. They called attention to racism and questioned the merits of assimilation.

As the studio system took hold of Hollywood in the second decade of the twentieth century, Young Deer lost control and was pushed to the sidelines, eventually disappearing from the movie world. After her career ended, St. Cyr worked in vaudeville, carved out a niche as a public lecturer, and became an advocate for American Indians.*

* A fuller account of the careers of James Young Deer and Princess Red Wing can be found in Philip Deloria, *Indians in Unexpected Places* (Lawrence, Kans.: University Press of Kansas, 2004).

The Vanishing American, which starred Richard Dix and debuted in theaters in 1925, lamented the treatment of indigenous people in the reservation system. Dix played a college-educated Native American who is forced to choose between accepting the ways of mainstream Anglo-American society or following the ways of his Native American heritage.

often entire encampments sponsored by individual shows, were featured in many silent films; on the other hand, figures like Buffalo Bill produced important films that laid the foundation for the western. Perhaps most notable was Cody's *The Indian Wars* (1914); filmed on the site of the Wounded Knee Massacre at the start of WWI, it received the endorsement of the War Department and pitted U.S. soldiers against descendants of the victims of the massacre in a triumphant re-creation. Moreover, emerging talents also made a name for themselves by making Indian-themed films during the silent era. D.W. Griffith, for instance, made *Pueblo Legend* (1912), *Massacre* (1912), and the influential *Battle at Elderbrush Gulch* (1914), which in retrospect looks like a template for later stories of Indian/white conflict on the frontier. Finally, especially after WWI, epic melodramas appeared that dramatized the plight of the American Indian. *The Vanishing American* (1925) is a classic expression of this sympathetic zeal, a film that critiques the treatment of indigenous people in the reservation system, while lamenting their impending doom.

THE MODERN WESTERN

The end of the silent era did not mark the end of Hollywood's fascination with Indians or Indian themes. In fact, by the early 1940s and through the 1960s, studios and audiences seized on the frontier, particularly conflicts between Native Americans and Euro-Americans to retell American history, rally public sentiments, and comment on important social issues. In television shows like the *Lone Ranger* (1949–1957) and seemingly countless movies, the West served as a backdrop for contemporary concerns. The western most often encouraged many Americans to view the settling of the West as a struggle between savagery and civilization. Films like *Stagecoach* (1939) painted indigenous peoples as marauding warriors, intent to destroy property, dash dreams, and kill settlers. Such films ultimately justified the dispossession and removal of Native nations (whether through relocation or extermination). Other films during this period created conflict between Native Americans and Euro-Americans for patriotic ends. For example, the story of Rogers' Rangers in *Northwest Passage* (1940) and the restaging of the Battle of the Little Bighorn in *They Died with Their Boots On* (1942) sought to rally Americans in the midst of the Second World War. At the same time, the western also allowed for more sympathetic, if not critical, assessments. Both *Broken Arrow* (1950) and *Cheyenne Autumn* (1964) lamented the fate of the once-proud people who originally inhabited the land, but importantly, could not waiver from the myth of the frontier or break with the inevitability of white triumph.

A NEW ERA

In the 1960s, the western began to die a slow death. Struggles for civil rights and social justice, combined with the war in Vietnam and the rapid pace of decolonization, made it increasingly difficult to celebrate last stands and cavalry charges or to replay cowboys and Indians. Moreover, the resurgence of Native America, including a cultural renaissance in the arts, literature, and political resistance, embodied famously by the American Indian Movement and the occupation of Alcatraz, challenged public perceptions and Hollywood imagery that had for so long painted Indians as simple, bellicose savages trapped in the past or doomed to vanish. As a consequence, the major films released in the late 1960s and early 1970s presented novel stories, ones that reworked the cinematic image of Indians. Whereas *Little Big Man* (1970) sought to retell American history, offering more progressive representations of Native Americans, other films used the Indian as an allegory for other social issues: *Tell Them Willie Boy Is Here* (1969) offered commentary on race relations in America and *Soldier Blue* (1970) used the Indian wars of the nineteenth century to critique U.S. involvement in Southeast Asia. At the same time, other films, most notably *A Man Called Horse* (1970), reiterated classic stereotypes of the savagery projected onto indigenous cultures.

For much of the next decade, the Hollywood Indian was on hiatus. Only slowly and intermittently in the 1980s did Indians and Indian themes return to the silver screen. While *First Blood* reintroduced the proud, resistant warrior, in its lead character, Rambo, who claimed Indian heritage, a remake of *Stagecoach* (1986) restaged the clichés of the western for a new generation. More importantly, two quirky movies broke with the past. *Powwow Highway* (1988) told a contemporary story of two Northern Cheyenne men, one (Philbert Bono) seeking to make traditional ways powerful in the modern world, and the other (Buddy Red Bow) fighting exploitation by U.S. government agencies and corporate interests, who set out on a journey to rescue Red Bow's sister and in the process find themselves, a strong bond, and how to be Indian in the modern world. The same year, *War Party* was released. It too was set in the present. The plot follows three young Blackfeet men who confront racism, challenge stereotypes, and flee a posse after inadvertently shooting a white man during the reenactment of a historic battle. Both films offer progressive, if flawed, portraits of Indians and Indian life. Unfortunately, they each cast non-Indian actors for some of the leading Indian roles. And worse, they remain isolated instances of the entertainment industry representing indigenous individuals and their issues in the contemporary world.

Coinciding with the five hundredth anniversary of Columbus' landing in the Caribbean, the Hollywood Indian has experienced something of a rebirth. While multiculturalism and an increased awareness of, if not sensitivity to, difference, promised to offer fuller, more human renderings of Native Americans, sadly, many mainstream images traveled backward in time and tone to speak to audiences in the present. On television, *Dr. Quinn Medicine Woman* retold the history of the frontier in romanticized terms, while *Twin Peaks* and *Northern Exposure* featured prominent indigenous characters in modern, if eccentric, settings. On the silver screen, with three exceptions, the crime drama *Thunderheart* (1992), the laughable *Last of the Dogmen* (1995), and the WWII action picture *Windtalkers* (2002), movies over the past fifteen years have told sweeping historical epics of cultural contact, unavoidable conflict, and impending doom. On the one hand, films like *Black Robe* (1992) and *Dances with Wolves* (1990) sought to render sympathetic and accurate historical portraits. On the other hand, *Pocahontas* (1995) and the latest remake of *Last of the Mohicans* (1993) exemplify the turn to the historical romance as a way to retell stories about the founding of America, the transcendent power of love, and commonalities across cultural boundaries. Indigenous actors were featured prominently and Native languages were spoken on screen. Still, white actors and actions took center stage in the movies, which had in common a nostalgic longing for Indian life before the coming of the white man. Consequently, at the start of the twenty-first century, much had changed in how the entertainment industry represented Native Americans, but much more had also remained the same.

MOVIE THEMES AND TRENDS

As this overly brief history of Indians and Indian themes in the movies and on television suggests, the portrayal of Native American cultures and histories has rarely, if ever, been fair, accurate, or reflective of indigenous perspectives. Instead, in these media, depictions of American Indians have relied on well-worn clichés. In this section, some of the most important ways indigenous peoples and their interactions with whites and white society have been represented in television and film and how these have changed over the past century will be addressed.

The Hollywood Indian, like its ancestor in literature, public policy, and popular thought, has taken many forms, which all have in common difference and savagery. Rennard Strickland (Osage-Cherokee), the former dean of the University of Oregon School of Law, has suggested that a pervasive feature of the entertainment industry

> . . . is the repetitive regularity of the image in movies that refines and reinforces the societal stereotypes. Hollywood provides an endless parade in which we have "good Indians and bad Indians." In the thousands of individual films and the millions of frames in those films, we have few, if any, "real Indians" who have individuality or humanity; who have families; who lead real lives that differ in marked degree from the lives of other "Indians." Hollywood has tried to

squeeze all of these people into these two basic molds. Almost five hundred tribes, bands, and villages are thus reduced to the homogenized film Indian stereotypes.[8]

Movies have used these basic templates to fashion four distinct Indian characters. First, the noble savage, reflecting Enlightenment preoccupations and romantic ideals, is child of nature, a spiritual creature, and a proud warrior, endowed with superhuman strength, grace, and bravery. The noble savage made intermittent appearances until becoming the preferred model for rendering Indianness in the 1990s. Excellent examples of the noble savage include the Lakotas in *Dances with Wolves* and Cochise in *Broken Arrow*. Second, the somewhat less noble, but praiseworthy sidekick is noteworthy for his willingness to assist and sacrifice for white heroes. Undoubtedly, Tonto of the *Lone Ranger* series epitomizes this character. Third, the ignoble savage is arguably the most common sort of Hollywood Indian. A warrior, frequently on horseback, often from the plains, the ignoble savage has been pictured as resistant, stoic, marauding, treacherous, amoral, and barbaric. A determined enemy of white settlers and soldiers alike, he is the subhuman counterpart to the noble savage. The entertainment industry has not tired of the ignoble savage over the past century, conjuring him time and again, from the anonymous Indians in *Battle at Elderbrush Gulch* to the Pawnee adversaries in *Dances with Wolves*. Finally, it must be noted that the Hollywood Indian has been decidedly male, only occasionally giving indigenous women more than a sideways glance, and then, almost invariably as the mythic Indian princess, including Sonseeahray in *Broken Arrow* and the title character in *Pocahontas*.

Language has always played a powerful role in representing indigenous peoples in films and television programs. The entertainment industry has often silenced Native Americans, representing them as stoic, unspeaking, aloof individuals. Equally common, these media have underscored the supposed inferiority of American Indians through their use and control of the English language: Indian characters regularly have spoken in broken English, marked by improper conjugation, fragmented phrases, and clichés. Less often, filmmakers used indigenous languages. At their worst, these were inadequately or improperly translated and even made up—as in *Scouts to the Rescue* (1939), in which English dialogue was played backward as an Indian language. More recently, it has become common for filmmakers to incorporate indigenous languages, as in *Black Robe* and *Dances with Wolves*, providing subtitles for English-speaking audiences. This is a hopeful sign.

Films and television programs also have relied on time to imagine Indians. With few exceptions, they have confined indigenous peoples to the past, literally freezing them in time. Specifically, they have focused on fictional and factual conflicts between Native Americans and Euro-American settlers, soldiers, and society. Such representations suggest that Native nations were static and unchanging. In contrast to Indians who are stuck in time as symbols of the past, whites are dynamic, embodying change, progress, and the future. In only rare instances have these media told stories about Indians as individuals who live in the present. Importantly, such portrayals have emerged only recently and then intermittently. Whereas mainstream cinema in the 1980s produced *Powwow Highway* and *War Party*, before returning to historic epics in the 1990s, television programs, like *Twin Peaks* and *Northern Exposure*, introduced recurring Indian characters. Undoubtedly, this pattern reflects the unresolved contradictions of American history and the fundamental importance of mythologizing relations with the indigenous peoples of North America. The more recent retrenchment, moreover, likely mirrors broader conservative shifts in American culture.

The Hollywood Indian has long been pictured more natural than his white counterpart, living in greater harmony with the natural world. While this arguably enhanced the savagery projected upon indigenous cultures from the silent era up

Northern Exposure, which aired on CBS from 1990 to 1995, was one of the first non-western television series to have recurring Native characters. Elaine Miles, who played Marilyn Whirlwind on the show, is Cayuse-Nez Perce and grew up on the Umatilla Reservation near Pendleton, Oregon.

through the golden age of the western, at least since the late 1960s, the environmental sensibilities imagined to be part of Native life have proven instrumental to a romantic recasting of the noble savage. The ecological Indian has captured many recent movies, most notably in *Dances with Wolves* and *Pocahontas.* Even though the connection between Indians and nature is cast in positive terms, it is important to note that such images are stereotypes that limit the humanity of indigenous peoples to a small set of attributes, qualities, and capacities, and should be seen as just as debilitating as ideas that appear negative and harmful.

Films and television programs with Indian themes also have offered interpretations of whites and white society. Not surprisingly stories told by whites to a largely white audience have validated Euro-American values and actions, casting whites as the central focus and animating force. In the stories told through these media, whites emerged not only as the righteous heroes, battling nature and savagery to establish law, order, and civilization; but they also have been portrayed as the victims of unwarranted attacks and unjustified treachery at the hands of Indians. Together, this imagery of heroism, civilization, victimization, and savagery transform the repeated invasions and encroachments of white settlers, which resulted in dispossession and conflict, into innocent and appropriate actions. The story of white America becomes a tale of virtuous, even determined, action, rather than a complex and contradictory narrative attentive to struggle, exploitation, and appropriation. In movies and television programs, moreover, whites regularly "go Native." From *The Last of the Mohicans* to *Dances with Wolves*, they express a fascination for indigenous life and customs, and more importantly integrate themselves in a Native culture. In essence, whites become Indians, adopted and accepted as equals by indigenous communities. While such romantic tales often suggest that whites are better Indians (more faithful to tradition and more adept at traditional practices) than the Indians themselves, they also offer a nostalgic critique of white society and its mores, arguing that more authentic and truer ways of being and belonging in the world could be found in indigenous life-ways. Thus, whites are not only cast in a good light as champions of civilization, but also give voice to negative assessments of modern life. Most often, a single, obvious bad white man, for instance Indian Agent

Booker in *The Vanishing American* and General George Armstrong Custer in *Little Big Man,* embodies the problems, excesses, and crimes of civilization. Such a narrative device again deflects attention from the systematic process and social ideologies that give life to history and cultural conflict. Whether heroes or villains, almost all portrayals of whites place Euro-American perspectives and peoples at the center of these media, forcing indigenous peoples and alternative perspectives to the margins.

Too often, the overarching message of films and television programs concerned with Native Americans and their interactions with whites and white society is that American Indians were (or are) doomed to vanish. This theme filtered into film from literature, perhaps notably in *The Last of the Mohicans,* which ends with the extinction of a Native nation, and under the influence of social Darwinist thought, as in *The Vanishing American,* with its tableau of evolutionary stages and assertion that indigenous people will assimilate or die. It emerged repeatedly in westerns that celebrated conquest, settler culture, and manifest destiny. More recently, it has been reworked again in romantic and remorseful tones: first as filmmakers and the broader public reconsidered and lamented the past treatment of Indians, as in *Little Big Man,* and then, as the tragic destiny of a proud people, as in *Dances with Wolves.* Even movies about love, rather than war and conflict, have turned on the demise and disappearance of Native Americans. Interracial intimacies invariably turn out badly for Indian characters. Rather than living happily ever after, they die as a result of their love across the color-line. Such is the sad fate of Sonseeahray in *Broken Arrow* and Uncas in *Last of the Mohicans.* Whether in proud defense of land and tradition, in the wake of civilization, or in the name of love, the Hollywood Indian, in sharp contrast to actual indigenous peoples, is destined to vanish.

Perhaps one reason the images of Native Americans and the accounts of American history offered in television programs and movies have remained so constant, in spite of shifting social circumstances and changing ideas about cultural difference, has been the entertainment industry itself. Indeed, how films have been produced and consumed has much to do with the persistence of anti-Indian stories and stereotypes. Importantly, while a few American Indians directed movies during the silent era, they played almost no role in the production of mainstream cinema until the making of *Powwow Highway* (which was based on a novel by Huron David Seals) in the 1980s and *Smoke Signals* in the 1990s (written by Sherman Alexie and directed by Chris Eyre). As a consequence, virtually every movie and television program made over the past century have been made by Euro-American writers, directors, and producers. Moreover, until the 1980s, it was common for Native American characters, especially central characters (heroes, villains, and love interests), to be portrayed by white actors in make-up. Likewise, the audience for television programs and movies centering on Americans Indians and their interactions with mainstream society has been overwhelmingly white. Even as it became increasingly common to employ Native American consultants, the intentions and objectives of the white-dominated film industry often supersede the advice and guidance of indigenous experts and elders. In the making of *Pocahontas*, for instance, Disney ignored Powhatan advisors, who stressed the historical realities of Euro-American conquest and the inappropriateness of transforming the prepubescent Pocahontas into a nubile princess, in an effort to craft an entertaining and profitable story. In the process, they created a film, according to Robert Eaglestaff, a Native American educator and principal in Seattle, that would unsettle creators and consumers alike if they saw it like many indigenous people did: it is "like trying to teach about the Holocaust and putting in a nice story about Anne Frank falling love with a German officer."[9] As a consequence of who has made, marketed, and watched these media, almost invariably, they have given voice to accepted understandings of the race, history, settling of the frontier, and Indian-white relations, while excluding indigenous voices and perspectives.

THE IMPACT OF HOLLYWOOD IMAGES

Although one might argue that the stories told about Indians, the frontier, and America are simple entertainment, such false, stereotypical renderings, so central to movies and television for so long, are far from harmless. Indeed, what makes televisual and cinematic representations of Native American cultures and histories so important is that they have shaped perceptions, practices, and policies. They have encouraged misrecognition of American Indians, warping understandings of their lives, capacities, values, and cultures. Movies and films have repeatedly reiterated that Native Americans are inhuman "others," alternately subhuman and superhuman, but always beyond the pale of civilization. If indigenous peoples are represented and accepted as inhuman, moreover, they cannot be seen to have genuine concerns, warrant equality, deserve respect, and merit inclusion in civil society. Worse, the persistence of anti-Indian interpretations in movies and on television have perpetuated cultural violence against Native nations, while establishing the groundwork for mistreatment, discrimination, and ethnic violence. Distorted understandings of culture and history continue to justify the conquest of Native America, contribute to denial of genocide, and reject the vitality of indigenous sovereignty.

More disturbing, movies and television not only make Native Americans and their concerns incomprehensible to a broader public, but they also negatively impact indigenous peoples. The prominence of these media and their reliance on distorted images of indigenous peoples and their historical relationships with mainstream society suggest that in consuming stories and stereotypes in these media, American Indians learn powerful lessons, some of which they surely internalize. Consequently, films and television encourage Native

Americans to misrecognize themselves. On the one hand, they may come to applaud the Hollywood Indian, seeing it as an acceptable representation of themselves. Some Apaches praised Ron Howard's reborn western *The Missing* for its portrayal of their culture, despite the fact that the film reduced Apache life and customs to violence, magic, and transgression, embodied in the villainous antagonist who takes pleasure in and makes a fortune raiding homesteads and enslaving white women.[10] On the other hand, cinematic and televisual images injure the self-image and self-esteem of indigenous youth. In fact, some have suggested that the ubiquity of such stories and stereotypes contributes to the frequency with which Indian youth attempt suicide and drop out from high school. Ultimately, movies and television programs with Indian themes have distorted and disempowered Native Americans.

SUMMARY

Nearly a century after American Indians began protesting their depiction in film, directors, producers, and writers still have not gotten the message. They have failed to listen to them or act on their concerns. To be sure, much has changed in how television and film represent American Indians. Nevertheless, as much as things have changed, more often than not the stories and stereotypes have persisted. More importantly, and arguably a key cause of the continuing misrepresentation of Native American cultures and history in Hollywood, American Indians remain on the margins of the television and film industry, all too often excluded from creating and controlling images. At the same time, the stereotypes and stories comprising the Hollywood Indian have been profitable and entertaining. This is because the American public needs myths about themselves, specifically stories and symbols that allow them to reconcile a past marked by forced removal, ethnoviolence, cultural repression, and demands that Indians assimilate with the ideals many believe make America great and unique, including liberty, equality, and opportunity. In the end, films and television programs with Indian themes should remind us that the entertainment industry remains overwhelming white and that its messages are made largely by, for, and about whites. Consequently, the Indians seen on the screen are not real, but projections, the white man's Indian, who always has said more about Euro-American issues, ideals, and identities than indigenous values, concerns, or cultures.

3

Journalistic Coverage

At the 2004 Grammy Awards, the popular hip-hop group Outkast staged their hit song "Hey Ya." The extravagant performance was enthusiastically received by the musicians, industry executives, and celebrities in attendance. Almost immediately, Native Americans watching expressed dismay over the misuse and misrepresentation of indigenous traditions and peoples. In letters to Native newspapers, online discussion forums, and official statements from political and cultural organizations, they noted that the group sampled a sacred Navajo song meant to heal veterans in the opening; incorporated a tepee as a prop; dressed in garish green attire, complete with bright fluffs and feathers designed to "look Indian"; danced in a suggestive fashion; and brought a marching band, wearing full headdresses, on stage at the climax of the act. Less than two weeks after Janet Jackson's "wardrobe malfunction" during the Superbowl halftime show, one might have expected the media to be attuned to representation, particularly on live television. Instead, few journalists seemed to notice the performance or the ensuing outrage in Indian Country. The lack of coverage led the Native American Journalists Association (NAJA) to issue a strongly worded press release, aimed at their peers in the mainstream media. It read in part:

> This is news, this is a story—one quickly recognized by the Native media. But where was the coverage? Where was the inquisitive media, sensitive to the communities they cover? Native peoples are not artifacts living in a museum that can be trotted out to entertain. They are living people whose pain is alive and perpetuated by actions—and the confounding lack of reaction by those who claim to know better.[11]

Importantly, NAJA condemns the lack of coverage and connects it with a broader history and a more general attitude.

The lack of coverage of the Outkast performance and the subsequent response across Native America reminds us that to the mainstream media American Indians, in and of themselves, are unimportant, unworthy of attention and engagement. Moreover, the failure to adequately report events and opinions in this context suggests that Native Americans are not seen as people, and that their concerns are not legitimate. Sadly, how the news media covered the outrage over the Outkast performance typifies journalist reporting on American Indians. Shaped by stereotypical understandings, the selection of subjects, point of view, and even word choice have conveyed a deep Euro-American bias to a broader public.

The reaction of NAJA underscores the affinity and connection between cinematic and journalistic portrayals of American Indians. Indeed, in common with the Hollywood Indian, the history of the newspaper Indian displays marked progress, becoming less overtly racist, if not embracing fair and balanced accounts of Native American cultures. Moreover, much like films and television, stereotyping and bias persist in journalism, casting a long shadow over the humanity of indigenous peoples, no less than the medium itself. Finally, as in the movies, journalist coverage has tended to speak for and about American Indians, denying them voice and full citizenship.

For all of the similarities with the Hollywood Indian, the newspaper Indian has displayed two important differences. First, whereas cinema has centered on Native Americans, granting them an exaggerated visibility, the news media too often have neglected American Indians, attending to their issues intermittently, and then only as they intersect with white society. Furthermore, the images and stereotypes that have overpopulated the silver screen are easy to trivialize and dismiss because they are fictional. In contrast, journalism hinges on truth, objectivity, and reporting on the real world. Consequently, the biased stories in newspapers and the evening news have had a more forceful impact on opinion and policy.

In this chapter, the outline and character of the newspaper Indian is addressed. First, an overview of the history of journalistic coverage, stressing the profound biases that have shaped news reporting and public understandings of Native Americans, is presented. Against this background, the current coverage of indigenous peoples, noting the structural and symbolic limitations of the news media, is detailed.

HISTORICAL OVERVIEW OF THE NEWSPAPER INDIAN

Print media were of the utmost importance to the creation of America's sense of itself in the nineteenth century. Newspapers, in particular, not only kept people informed of events and issues, but connected individuals in a common public culture. Significantly, over the course of the nineteenth century American journalism became a modern profession, evolving from a highly politicized and less formal means to disseminate ideas and opinions to a vocation committed to objectivity, truth, and the public, as journalism replaced lay correspondence.

Native Americans have never been a central focus of the news media. In fact, they make appearances in newspapers (and later on the radio and television) invariably when they clash with white society. Not surprisingly, given that most reporters have been white and subscribed (in whole or in part) to the ideals and attitudes of American society, American Indians have rarely been represented as people (though perhaps this has occurred with greater frequency over the past forty years). Instead, they have been shadows of themselves, mirrors for the dominant society, scapegoats for settlers, and victims of progress, precisely because journalists, unaware, miseducated, and at times maliciously, have represented them through stereotypes. Indeed, for much of the first century and a half of American journalism, newspapers almost exclusively offered terribly negative images of indigenous peoples that can only be described as expressions of anti-Indian racism. Increasingly over the course of the twentieth century, the evil subhuman warrior has been joined, if not replaced altogether by other stereotypes (the drunk, the impoverished, the ward of the state, or the traditional), some which actually purport to empathize with American Indians (the victim, the mystic, the shaman, or the activist).

The Nineteenth Century

In the nineteenth century, the news media was anything but fair or impartial. It offered prejudiced, if not overtly racist, accounts of American Indians and their actions. Although more urgent and vitriolic along the western frontier, newspapers across the country used stories about Native Americans to advance political agendas and arguments for particular policies. Its flat and regularly false images also afforded editors opportunities to lampoon and critique mainstream institutions and ideas. Above all else, the encounters and conflicts between Native Americans and Euro-Americans, Natives and settlers, and warriors and soldiers became lucrative, selling papers and securing support for U.S. military action.

THREE INDIAN CAMPAIGNS. 731

IN THE WAKE OF THE DESTROYER.

scouted the mountains in every direction, giving the hostiles no chance to attack the settlements.

Before long, runners came in to the San Carlos from the scattered tribe, asking for peace and permission to return. The commanding general met every such messenger with the information that any band might come in which would surrender one or all of four outlaws named. These were Chontz, Cochenay, Pedro, one of the most active leaders in the murders on the river of that name, and Sondazzy, the tool of Chontz in the killing, a short time before, of a cavalry officer at the agency. They were also notified that if they could not surrender the outlaws named alive, they themselves should mete out the punishment of death, and that upon proof that a just fate had overtaken the desperate criminals, any and all the other Indians could come in and live at peace.

So it finally turned out: the Indians themselves punished the outlaws, furnishing satisfactory proof that justice had been done, and before summer the Arivipa tribe was re-established at the San Carlos Agency.

With an account of one other event of Indian warfare, which gives a phase of

Excerpts from Wesley Merritt's *Three Indian Campaigns* appeared in *Harper's Monthly* in 1890. This illustration, which accompanies the excerpt, was typical of the way American Indians were portrayed in the late 1800s—as savage marauders, bent on raiding and killing Anglo settlers.

The sensational coverage of the clash of cultures centered around a singular, stereotypical figure, the bad Indian, an evil hostile, a savage marauder, a warrior on horseback beyond the pale of civilization. In countless stories, the savage warrior attacked innocent settlers, raided unprotected encampments, and threatened the rule of law and order. Headlines warned of impending massacres; articles recounted the miserable fate of unfortunate settlers; editorials encouraged stronger action. Even incidents that best illustrate the terror and atrocities associated with the spread of settlers and soldiers were spun to grant Euro-Americans victory through valor and blame the victims for imagined transgressions. Reporting of the Battle of the Little Bighorn, still better known as Custer's Last Stand, in 1876, transformed what was to be a surprise military raid by the Seventh U.S. Cavalry upon an encampment of Lakotas and Cheyennes into a massacre of an America hero at the hands of inhumane savages. Worse, the coverage of the Ghost Dance spiritual movement cast it as an uprising. As a consequence of "inaccurate, sensational, and inflammatory" reporting, including fake sources and forged eyewitness accounts that were little more than propaganda, the Seventh U.S. Cavalry's action (some say revenge) against an unarmed Lakota encampment that killed scores of men, women, and children became justified.[12] Portraying the American Indian as an evil savage, hostile to civilization and settlers, not only advocated for the rule of law, but made acceptable campaigns of death and destruction directed at Native Americans.

Indeed, news reporting reflected settler sentiments, validating their encroachment, righteousness, and low opinion of indigenous peoples, and more importantly, it frequently inflamed them as well. The Camp Grant Massacre offers a tragic example of this pattern. As tension rose between residents of Tucson, Arizona, and local Apaches, all three of the local papers fanned white racism and hostility toward the Indians at Grant Camp. Shortly before the massacre, the

Weekly Arizona outlined the preferred course of action: "receive them when they apply for peace, and have them grouped together and slaughtered as though they were so many rattlesnakes."[13] At the same time, the *Arizonan* encouraged white residents to offer Apaches "a slight entertainment to the music of about a hundred double-barreled shotguns. We are positive such a course would produce the best results." Not surprisingly, such anti-Indian, dehumanizing rhetoric contributed to a spasm of ethnic cleansing: a week later, white settlers killed one hundred Apaches, many of them women and children.

Not all journalistic renderings of Native Americans were hostile. In fact, more sympathetic images and understandings of American Indians did appear on the pages of newspapers. Far less common than its hostile counterpart, the journalistic version of the good Indian reworked the romantic notion of the noble savage: on occasion it embraced indigenous beliefs and behaviors as equally human, if not superior, on others it praised the American Indian character, including attributes like kindness, wisdom, pride, and bravery, but most often to defend Native Americans from mistreatment or to critique U.S. government policy. Perhaps one of the greatest ironies of more sympathetic coverage of Native Americans was that it often had detrimental consequences as well. In the context of Indian Removal, for instance, "The sympathetic press, like the anti-Indian press cleared the way" for the displacement of the southern tribes "by corroborating the idea of the vanishing Indian and advocating for a paternalistic attitude toward Indian life."[14]

Throughout the nineteenth century, newspapers fashioned and refashioned Indianness as the social and political circumstances demanded, but they never tired of the hostile savage:

> Violent encounters between evil Indians and innocent whites made compelling, page-one stories; peaceful relations and gentle Indians did not. Moreover, Indian-white conflicts

could be easily reduced to a standard set of sensational "facts," ready-made for telegraphic transmission . . . Even when "good" Indians were featured in the papers, their stories lacked the vivid details necessary to capture the public imagination . . . For Native Americans, already viewed as savage and uncivilized, this emphasis on violence worked to reinforce Indian inferiority.[15]

And, it is this legacy of racism, exaggerated violence, and politically motivated misrepresentations that continue to haunt the mainstream news media down to the present as it tries to reimagine the newspaper Indian.

The Twentieth Century

Whereas nineteenth-century journalism, when it attended to Native America, was preoccupied with military campaigns and settlers' struggles against evil Indians, twentieth-century news media would prove no more attentive, but would begin to soften its portrayal of American Indians. In fact, although journalistic bias would lessen only after 1960, and then only partially, an often romanticized newspaper Indian would be conjured intermittently in conjunction with broader social upheaval and largely to salve white fears and guilt.

Increasingly after 1920, perhaps in response to the patriotic service of many American Indians, a sea of change swept across public opinions about Native American issues, fostering more sympathetic, if no less stereotypical, images. The good Indian came to the fore. Journalistic coverage casting the tensions between assimilation and pluralism in exotic tones contributed to both continuity and change during this period. In fact, up until the Second World War, journalistic coverage eschewed grounded reporting and analysis, favoring instead "nostalgia, sentimentality, romance, or humor."[16] Reporting on religion, for instance, made it a cross "between a circus act and a museum exhibit." More generally, warriors faded to the background and were replaced by noble savages.

A clear example of the new framing of Indianness can be seen in reporting on a bill proposed by Republican Senator Holm Olaf Bursum of New Mexico to settle Pueblo Indian land claims to the decided advantage of white settlers, while undermining Pueblo sovereignty. Although a small number of stories suggested that the Pueblo Indians were lazy, the bulk of the news coverage depicted them as good Indians, children of nature who were spiritually superior. A story in the *New York Times* in 1923 praised them, drawing clear parallels between American ways and those of the Pueblo Indians:

> They are brave and splendid fighters but their wars . . . always have been on the defensive. They are peacefully inclined . . . The Pueblos have always been farmers . . . They are monogamists . . . The Pueblo's wife is the mistress of the house in every sense of that word. Reverence for their women is almost a religion to them. No white parents are more tender in their care of their children than the Pueblos.[17]

Others, like Charles A. Selden in the *Ladies' Home Journal,* spoke in even more romantic terms:

> No Pueblo housewife ever had nervous prostration. What American women . . . are frantically groping for in their pursuit of one strange cult after another is . . . peace of mind, The Indian woman has that as a matter of course . . . [Pueblos] are inferior no doubt in mechanical industry and money getting. In things of the spirit they are equal to the best of us and superior to most.[18]

In part, the overwhelmingly approving language used to describe the Pueblos and their resistance to assimilation derived from a conception of them as an ancient and traditional people that a society devoted to pluralism should respect. In large measure because of the mainstream media coverage, supporters of the Bursum Bill were forced to compromise.

When the United States entered the Second World War, news coverage moved away from exotic imagery. Journalists returned to the figure of the warrior, using it to celebrate Native Americans. They reincarnated the noble savage, dressing him in the uniform of the U.S. armed forces. For much of the decade, Native Americans would be praised for their patriotism and bravery. For instance, in an article published in *Collier's*, "Indians have a name for Hitler," Secretary of Interior Harold L. Ickes remarked, Native soldiers have "endurance, rhythm, a feeling for timing, co-ordination, sense perception, an uncanny ability to get over any sort of terrain at night, and, better than all else, an enthusiasm for fight."[19] Their participation in the war effort was matched by media portrayals that include them more fully in American society, routinely depicting them as exemplifying American ideals. Correspondent Ernie Pyle filed the following dispatch on the eve of the landing at Okinawa:

> Before the convoy left . . . the Navajos . . . put on a ceremonial dance. The Red Cross furnished some colored cloth and paint to stain their faces and they made up the rest of their Indian costumes from chicken feathers, sea shells, coconuts, empty ration cans, and rifle cartridges. Then they did their own ceremonial chants and dances under the tropical palm trees with several thousand marines as a grave audience. In their chant they asked the great gods in the sky to sap the Japanese of their strength . . . they ended their ceremonial chant by singing the Marine Corps song in Navajo.[20]

For a brief moment, the news media spoke of Native Americans in sympathetic and celebratory tones, which also revived the stereotypes associated with the noble savage.

Perhaps because of the reporting in the 1940s, politicians embraced Termination, or the abrogation of American Indian treaties, as a way to advance the American way. During this period, the good Indian was not the warrior or the exotic traditional. Instead, "the 1950s good Indian was someone who fitted in."[21] Media coverage offered extremely negative and judgmental assessments of American Indians. They were presented as wasteful and lazy, too often unwilling to assimilate. A 1953 article in *Commonweal*, for instance, opined:

> Contact with the White man's world and the protracted sate of tutelage have inevitably weakened the Indian's society and sapped his moral fiber. These wards of the state have grown content with letting others take care of them. And when big money has come their way they have shown a talent for speedily throwing it to the four winds.[22]

Moreover, national media coverage excluded historical context and failed to analyze the policy shift, literally white-washing the news. Importantly, local coverage was often more humane, putting a human face on the policy and its implication.

After 1960, the political movements and cultural resurgence in Native America that called into question the content of the anti-Indian western also had important implications for the mainstream news media. Demands for self-determination and the quest for social justice initially met with ridicule. A *Newsweek* article, for instance, described the 1961 American Indian Conference in Chicago derisively:

> It was the first time since Hiawatha was knee-high to a tall papoose that braves grown gray and come from every tribe ... to sit around a mystical council fire. To indulge the White man's notion of the red man (and satisfy their own passion for ethnic distinction), they first passed around and puffed the calumet.[23]

Not long after this, journalism shifted its perspective, likely influenced by the civil rights movement, the push for a Great Society, and later rising protests against the Vietnam War. Indeed, not more than five years later, reporters had turned a sympathetic eye toward Indian Country, underscoring the social ills plaguing it, while reviving the noble savage in their rendering of indigenous peoples and traditions.

Even as they reevaluated who Indians were, the mainstream news media returned its gaze to conflict, specifically activism and a series of dramatic occupations in which political groups sought to make their concerns audible to a broader public. Initially, the news media portrayed the occupation of Alcatraz in 1969 as heroic: "The symbolic act of Indian awareness" and a "stunning act of the imagination and the will."[24] In turn, the activists responsible were rendered in glowing, even reverent, tones that praised their beauty, nobility, and intellect. As the eighteen-month occupation wore on, journalistic images and language darkened, stressing hostility, violence, and transgression. And the aftermath emphasized destruction. A similar pattern emerged in mainstream coverage of the taking of Wounded Knee, South Dakota, by members of the American Indian Movement in 1973. At first, the media offered a positive image of those occupying the town and the struggle in which they were engaged. Over time, however, most outlets, save perhaps for the *New York Times*, began to side with the U.S. government forces laying siege to the town. The resulting biased coverage read like that written by war correspondents. It painted the American Indian Movement (AIM) and its members as radicals and subversive, warriors best understood as violent and hostile. At these moments, the more positive regard of the press and the public reverted to anti-Indianism, and was little changed from the previous century and eerily familiar from Hollywood westerns.

The tensions within mainstream news coverage simultaneously romanticizing and demonizing American Indians, reflected the deep ambivalence with which Americans have long regarded Native Americans: good/bad, noble/savage, warrior/victim, and so on. Importantly, as the press struggled with these contradictions, it also worked to address the legacies of its own history. In part, this meant that the media opened itself to outside perspectives. They took the critiques of Native American leaders and activists seriously. Local television news directors and newspaper editors, as chapter 5 explores in greater detail, allocated time and space for American Indian voices. In some cases, they also established advisory boards to grant them a fuller understanding of Indian Country. At the same time, they endeavored to increase the presence and participation of American Indians in journalism.

The twentieth century witnessed a softening of media imagery and public attitudes toward American Indians. Nevertheless, stereotypes lingered, shaping coverage and representations to this day.

Contemporary Patterns

Clearly, the newspaper Indian has evolved over the past two hundred years; however, distorted imagery and biased coverage persist. Indeed, too often the mainstream news media still fails to provide accurate or adequate reporting on American Indians and their concerns. Outside of local papers, Native Americans remain largely invisible, because the news industry does not recognize them as significant. Surely, the small size of the indigenous population contributes to this, as does the faulty perception that Indians live only on reservations and in rural areas. Much more important, though, are the ways that popular attitudes and engrained cultural dispositions continue to limit the kind and quality of questions mainstream journalists, committed as they are to objectivity, the truth, and public good, might ask about American Indians.

Many reporters either are uninformed about central issues, such as sovereignty, identity, history, culture, diversity, and worldview, or worse, have been misinformed by popular culture and the superficial lessons imparted by well-meaning teachers and biased textbooks. As a consequence, news reporting regularly wrongly communicates situations and their significance to all who have a stake in them, and in the process do a disservice to their audience, reinforcing the systematic miseducation of the public—including future reporters—to American Indians, who often get lost in external understandings and agendas, and to dialogue about important issues from casinos and repatriation to the environment and child welfare. In some cases, journalism perpetuates damaging stereotypes about indigenous peoples. Although these tend to avoid demonizing Native Americans as evil or subhuman, they do invoke clichéd conceptions that limit their humanity. For instance, in common with the New Age reclamation of the Indian in popular culture generally, and Hollywood films (recall the discussion of *Pocahontas* and *Dances with Wolves*) specifically, reporting on Native Americans frequently accentuates their connection with nature or their inherent spirituality, traits deemed positive and noble, which they nevertheless romanticize and generalize in problematic ways.

Importantly, the nature of the contemporary mainstream news media contributes to these patterns as well. First, few American Indians participate in the industry, though there are notable exceptions, such as Emmy Award-winning television reporter Hattie Kauffman (Nez Perce) and longtime columnist and editor Mark N. Trahant (Shoshone-Bannock). In other words, the news media remains disproportionately white, tends to reside in urban areas, embraces modern values, leans to the left, and tacitly endorses Judeo-Christian values. This makes it difficult, if not impossible, for journalists to cover, let alone consider, stories about a marginal, ethnic minority, encompassing more than five hundred recognized tribes, whose members live on reservations, as well as in suburbs and slums; who accept and reject the American dream; and who defend, live, or have turned away from traditional spiritual practices. Second, the news cycle, in an increasingly commercial, global, and visual media, moves faster and faster, fostering short-term, if not superficial, reporting on an event or issue. This model, which might be described as hit-and-run journalism for a world on

Hattie Kauffman (Nez Perce) is the national news correspondent for CBS' *Early Show*. The native of Seattle, Washington, was the first Native American journalist to report on a national broadcast in 1989 and has won several Emmy Awards for her reporting.

the go, does not resonate well with the pace and practices in many American Indian communities. In social worlds, where people are rightfully suspicious of the media, may not have access to a telephone, and may not know the reporter, it is hard for journalists to establish relationships and rapport needed for good reporting. Third, competition for audience and profits encourages the mainstream news media to follow sensational stories that speak to the most people in the most rudimentary terms; at the same time, it discourages coverage of difficult, complex, and unfamiliar issues that demand sensitivity and patience. Together, these features of the mainstream news media work to exclude indigenous concerns and perspectives, while hampering understanding and dialogue about important social and political issues.

The structures and sentiments at the heart of the news media also limit the kinds of stories told about Native Americans. In an anecdotal critique, Joseph Allen, Rosebud Sioux photographer and publisher of the independent newspaper *The Circle*, suggests that American journalism tends to publish four kinds of stories about American Indians. First, the news media offers accounts of conflicts with white society, or what he terms, "Indians on the Warpath." Second, it renders "Pretty Powwow Pictures," which superficially and romantically capture Indianness through familiar symbols and ceremonies. Third, the news media like to tell stories that transpose Horatio Alger onto Indian Country in what he calls "From Rez Rags to Riches." And fourth, "the Little Indian that could" narrative allows white audiences to read about the struggles of individuals against racism, poverty, and tradition in the hope of making a difference. Clearly, the attention to conflict and noble savages tie current journalism to its past. The interest in individual success and the American dream, however, highlight the emergence of novel, if formulaic, storylines in the mainstream media.[25]

A recent study, cosponsored by the Native American Journalists Association and News Watch, confirms and extends Allen's observations.[26] "The Reading Red Report," which was written by Kara Briggs, Tom Arvison, Dennis McAuliffe, and Lori Edmo-Suppah, analyzed stories about American Indians or with Indian themes published between February 1, 1999, and February 1, 2002, in nine of the top ten newspapers in the United States: the *Chicago Sun-Times*,

Houston Chronicle, Los Angeles Times, New York Daily News, Newsday, New York Times, USA Today, Wall Street Journal, and *Washington Post.* During this period, the papers published 1,133 articles about American Indians. Although the stories covered a range of topics from cooking and the arts to Code Talkers and Indian-government relations, they clustered around four subjects. First, "on the res" stories were the most common, totaling 225. These articles offered accounts of American Indian life in the context most Americans associate with Indianness. Stories from Pine Ridge, South Dakota, and Window Rock, Arizona, dominated reporting in this category. Briggs and her colleagues lament the emphasis on these portrayals: "At worst, they reinforced stereotypes about barren landscapes, family feuds, and poor yet mystical people, the kind you might see in an old episode of 'Northern Exposure'."[27] Worse, now that the majority of Native Americans live in urban areas, eight of the nine papers neglected to report on the large number of American Indians living in their communities, even as they sent reporters to faraway reservations. Second, the major dailies published nearly 150 articles on tribal casinos. Rather than seriously or sensitively probe issues of sovereignty, economic success, or the meaning of gaming in Native communities, the stories stressed contentious efforts to gain approval for casinos and the details of bureaucratic procedures. Third, the newspapers published 116 stories on the controversies over mascots, which the authors deemed appropriate due to the disastrous consequences of stereotyping and racism, including weakened self-worth and even suicide. Fourth, 62 articles were written on the unfolding scandal surrounding the mismanagement of the American Indian Trust Fund by the Bureau of Indian Affairs (BIA). Briggs and her associates question both the intense focus on process and more importantly the extent of coverage, calling for more in light of the $10 billion under dispute.

Not surprisingly, "The Reading Red Report" found that

Indian Gaming and Media Stereotypes

In 1988, the U.S. Congress passed the Indian Gaming Regulatory Act, which allowed tribes to establish casinos. Dozens of tribes from Connecticut to California have opened gaming complexes in the intervening years.

Casinos have had decidedly positive benefits for Native nations and American society more generally. Tribes with gaming have enjoyed increased per-capita and household income and a drop in unemployment. At the same time, tribal casinos have produced thousands of jobs for non-Natives and millions of tax dollars for state and federal governments.

Despite these contributions, many Americans have stereotypes about Indians and Indian gaming. Public misconceptions often derive from and mirror media coverage. Indeed, while much of the news reporting on the subject is fair, biased reporting remains far too common, reinforcing anti-Indian racism.

Reporters and columnists rely on clichés to convey the nature of tribal casinos and perpetuate ugly, hurtful images of American Indians. In recent years, the media used phrases like "on the warpath," "war drums," and "Indian massacre" to describe the conflict over Indian gaming. Moreover, supporters of casinos and tribes have been maligned through racist rhetoric. One tribal lawyer in California was dubbed "Chief Running Mouth." And politicians receiving campaign funds from tribes with casinos, in turn, have found themselves debased through similarly charged language. Former California Governor Gray Davis was called a "pale-face" after "wampum," while Lieutenant Governor Cruz Bustamante was doing a "rain dance" for campaign funds.

Tribal casinos have fostered a series of misconceptions and misrepresentations about American Indians as well. In their accounts, journalists and commentators paint indigenous peoples as greedy, opportunistic, corrupt, and manipulative. At the same time, the opulence of gaming complexes has encouraged many to wrongly conjure "the rich Indian" to represent all Indians today. Casinos, moreover, have led many pundits and reporters to question the authenticity of both gaming and the tribes participating in it, suggesting that gambling is not really Indian and that many of the tribes are not real Indians.*

---

*   Many of the details in this sidebar come from Rob Schmidt, "The Facts about Indian Gaming, " which can be accessed at *http://www.bluecorncomics.com/gaming.htm.*

"prejudicial news coverage" thrives in the mainstream media.[28] Four areas concern them specifically. First, they note that journalists fail to consult Native Americans, repeating ideas and values central to the Western worldview. For instance, during the period under discussion nearly a dozen articles discussed the origins of American Indians; all looked to science for the answer, ignoring indigenous peoples and their accounts. Similarly, stories on archaeological assertions of prehistoric cannibalism failed to ask what would American Indians say and how they would feel about such findings. Second, word choice, like "discovery" to describe the exploits of Columbus or Lewis and Clark, according to the authors, remains problematic for accurate reporting and full understandings. Third, the choice of topics proved disturbing. The study identified some glaring stereotypes, including stories on alcoholics, the use of "Native wisdom" for weather casting, a "shopping trip" to gather a Native meal, and a second grade appreciation of Native American Heritage Month. The story lead for the latter clearly encapsulates the extent of the problem surveyed in "The Reading Red Report": "Welcome to The Tribe. You have to earn the feathers for your headdress in Chief Colorful Butterfly's classroom. And sometimes if you're naughty, you get your feathers plucked."[29] Fourth, headlines too often played off stereotypes. Examples include "Lakotas Last Stand" (referencing the Battle of the Little Bighorn) and "Could be time for another Powwow on this Issue" (to describe an ongoing mascot controversy). Finally, the news coverage detailed in the study reiterates the old pattern of almost exclusively considering American Indians only in relation to (and especially in conflict with) white society.

Importantly, the study underscored the strides made in mainstream journalism over the past forty years:

> The best stories simply reflected good-quality and fair-minded reporting, writing and editing applied to Native

America. They treated Americans as people rather than historical figures. They explained to readers the unique status of the 560 federally recognized tribal nations as sovereign governments within the United States. They acknowledged the depth and diversity of Native American communities.[30]

The report singled out reporting on endangered indigenous languages, the environmental legacies of General Motors for St. Regis Mohawks, and a musical collaboration between a classical music company from New York and the Kalispel tribe. Despite the persistence of misinformation, bias, and stereotypes, "The Reading Red Report" suggests that the future of Native Americans in the news is not destined to recycle the failings of the past.

SUMMARY

In 1958, legendary newsman Edward R. Murrow noted the dependence of mainstream media on the Hollywood Indian, stressing that it prevented journalists from accurately reporting on Native Americans:

> If Hollywood were to run out of Indians, the program schedules would be mangled beyond all recognition. Then some courageous soul with a small budget might be able to do a documentary telling what, in fact, we have done—and are still doing—to the Indians in this country.[31]

Unfortunately, Murrow overestimated the capacity of journalism to accurately and adequately document Native America or to discredit the Hollywood Indian. To be sure, reporters have rendered American Indians in sympathetic terms and the industry and profession have worked to welcome them; more often than not, however, the mainstream news media have offered biased accounts of Native Americans and their concerns that have stressed racial difference, violence, and savagery. Sadly, as recently as September 21, 2004, in the venerated

Wall Street Journal, Steven Kaplan shamelessly compared Iraq, Afghanistan, and countless unnamed fronts in the war on terror with Indian Country, arguing the twenty-first century army must adapt to face terrorists and insurgents around the world who threaten the American way of life, much as its old enemy, American Indian warriors, had on the western frontier in the nineteenth century.[32] As much as one might like to think the Newspaper Indian has faded into the past, the evil, marauding savage laying in await to harm innocent citizens and destroy civilization is very much alive and well.

4

Mascots

Although many Americans never give a second thought to the use of Indian names, symbols, and material culture in athletics, increasingly, Native American mascots have fostered controversy, protest, and conflict. The lyrics of "Mascot" by the indigenous hip-hop group Without Rezervations attest to the scope and significance of this conflict:

> I can't believe we're still on the sporting line,
> On the news each and every night.
> A Redskin massacre, a Braves scalping,
> Whose image do you think that's helping?[33]

During the course of the twentieth century, the use of Indian names, imagery, and cultural artifacts became a familiar feature of athletic competitions and an accepted way for fans, players, students, and alumni to identify themselves, their sport teams, and their communities. At the height of their popularity, Native American mascots represented more than a score of professional or semi-professional teams, more than one hundred institutions of higher education, and several thousand high schools across the United States. Beginning in the late 1960s, in association with broader civil rights movements and a cultural resurgence in Indian Country, such mascots became increasingly problematic. As a result, numerous schools and sports teams have ended their use of Indian symbols. In fact, Suzan Shown Harjo, director of the Morning Star Institute, has estimated that more than 1,500 Native American mascots have been retired over the past 35 years.

This chapter seeks to explain where Native American mascots came from and how they became a problem for schools and communities. At root, it aims to clarify what is at stake in the use of Indian imagery in athletics. Conflicts over mascots are not simply, as some would have it, instances of political correctness; rather, they invariably entail the meaning of history, belonging, and opportunity, revealing what it means to be an American.

INDIAN IMAGERY IN ATHLETICS

Native American mascots, despite the claims of some supporters, have never faithfully depicted Native cultures and histories, nor communicated the humanity of American Indians. Instead, relying on and recycling stereotypes, they have assembled what historian Robert Berkhofer dubbed, "the white man's Indian," an imaginary creature that is useful to white society but that has little or no connections to the realities of Native life.[34] Consequently, they misrepresent Native Americans, rendering them as partial, unreal, and less than human.

Native American mascots reduce indigenous peoples to fragments wrongly thought to encapsulate or describe them. Most often in the world of sports, Indian imagery breaks down the complexities of Native lives as lived, reassembling them through four dimensions: 1) physical features, invariably nose, skin color, or hair; 2) material culture, including buckskin,

The Tyranny of the Majority

Increasingly, politicians, school administrators, and journalists have turned to public opinion polls as a means of assessing Native American mascots. To date, the results of polls have displayed great variation and contradiction but nevertheless prove instructive. First, Euro-Americans are more likely than Native Americans to support Native American mascots. Second, the (over-whelming) majority of Euro-Americans endorse the use of Indian symbols and mascots. Third, Native Americans, like Euro-Americans, do not (nor should not be expected to) agree about mascots. Fourth, while many Native Americans disapprove of Native American mascots, other Native Americans are untroubled or even support them.

These patterns, in turn, raise fundamental questions.

To begin, how does public opinion about American Indian mascots matter? Would we settle concerns about other human rights issues or moral debates by taking a survey? For instance, if most Americans found nothing wrong with slavery, rape, or genocide, would that justify those practices? Unfortunately, attention to surveys tends to turn attention away from the moral concerns and human rights, reducing the tangible harms and the standing of others to matters of individual opinion, subject to dispute. Worse, supporters of such imagery often point to polling data—which suggests the majority of Americans find Native American mascots to be harmless, acceptable, or even respectful—to advance their claims that the controversy is unimportant, an invention of a vocal minority.

Of equal importance, what are we to make of the support for Native American mascots among some indigenous peoples? Many American Indians, exposed to the same media and messages as others in the United States, have internalized prevailing ideas and images: on the one hand, they may come to misinterpret Indianness, accepting popular fabrications as rea-sonable; on the other hand, they may settle for the available imagery because it is the only possibility that mainstream media affords them.

feathers, and/or headdress; 3) expressive forms, particularly dance and face painting; and 4) personality characteristics like stoicism or bravery. Moreover, Native American mascots trap indigenous peoples within well-worn clichés, derived from dime novels, Wild West shows, movies, scouting, and advertising. As a result, more often than not, such representations have more to do with Euro-American interpretations and preoccupations than with indigenous cultures. Indian imagery in sport, furthermore, tends to freeze Native Americans. Specifically, mascots confine indigenous peoples in the past (romanticized representatives from a golden age); they frequently restrict them to the plains (the Lakota and other nomadic horse cultures principally); and they refer to cultural conflict and military struggles between Euro-Americans and Native Americans. In the process, generic Indians emerge, which cannot be faithful to Native histories and traditions, precisely because what makes them possible, pleasurable, and powerful is reduction, fragmentation, exaggeration, and decontextualization.

Importantly, the invented Indians who dance at halftime, mark the stationery of educational institutions, and appear on baseball caps and T-shirts are of two types: the warrior and the clown, mirroring the historic bifurcation of indigenous people into two types of savages—noble and ignoble. The warrior aspires to honor. Stressing bravery and bellicosity, the warrior exudes the character traits Euro-Americans have long prized: individuality, perseverance, pride, fidelity, and excellence. Numerous high schools, colleges, and professional teams have seized upon the warrior, real—Chief Osceola at Florida State University—and imagined—Chief Illiniwek at the University of Illinois. In contrast, the less common clown mocks, making Indians a joke, or a sideshow burlesque. The Cleveland Indians' Chief Wahoo is likely the most recognizable clown.

History of Mascots
Euro-Americans began using Indian imagery in athletics at the

close of the nineteenth century. In part, they seized upon Indianness in response to a number of major societal shifts, including the close of the frontier, the end of armed conflict with indigenous peoples, the quickening of urbanization and industrialization, the prominence of social Darwinism and an associated push to assimilate Native Americans, the expansion of the American empire, and a crisis in what it meant to be and become a man. At the same time, Indian imagery emerged from a long tradition of playing Indian in the United States. At least since the Boston Tea Party, Euro-Americans have sought to recast themselves by adopting the customs, regalia, and visage they associated with Native Americans. Playing Indian, in the absence of embodied Indians, allowed them to fashion a uniquely American identity, distinguishing their young nation, underscoring its democratic values, independent spirit, and historic birthright. Later, precisely as schools and teams were donning Indian imagery, scouting, woodcraft, and similar movements took shape in an effort to cultivate, redirect, and even save young white men from the feminizing perils of modern civilization. Of equal importance is the romantic image of the warrior so frequently embraced in the creation of Native American mascots derived from dime novels, advertising, journalistic coverage of the Indian Wars, and later movies. These features also account for the pronounced tendency of such mascots to draw on popular correlations between Indians and particular horse cultures of the Plains region. Finally, the emergence of Native American mascots reflected the trajectory of the American empire: On the one hand, such mascots are trophies, the prize of conquest, replicating the propensity of settlers to take and remake Native places and practices without permission; on the other hand, they encourage citizens and communities to affirm who they are and where they came from—the rightful heirs of once-proud people who valiantly fought against a superior civilization.

Although informed by broader social and political forces,

the selection of Native American mascots has always been a local affair. At educational institutions, almost invariably, students seized upon and elaborated Indian imagery. For instance, at the University of Illinois, a student in the marching band, drawing on his fondness for Native Americans and his experience as a Boy Scout, invented the school's mascot, Chief Illiniwek. And, when Florida State University became a coeducational institution after the Second World War, students voted to adopt the Seminoles as the school mascot. Other schools, such as Dartmouth College, which once assigned itself the mission of educating Native Americans, built upon historic relationships with indigenous peoples in their decision to use Indian imagery. And some teams, including the Cleveland Indians and several high schools, attribute the origins of the name and mascot to a desire to honor a specific individual of Indian heritage who formerly played for or coached the team. Regional connections were also important. Marquette University dubbed itself the Warriors in the early 1950s, after the Boston Braves baseball team moved to Milwaukee. More commonly, high schools and colleges have sought to commemorate Native nations with a local connection. The Fighting Illini of the University of Illinois, the Seminoles of Florida State University, and the Running Utes of the University of Utah all attest to this pattern, suggesting, at least in part, that the choice of name is about claiming land and identity from the aboriginal inhabitants subsequently displaced and dispossessed with the establishment of state and school. Finally, some schools, like St. John's University and Simpson College, established traditions of playing Indian largely by accident, because of the colors of their uniforms or a newspaper article comparing the play of the team to the fighting prowess of Indians.

Controversy over Mascots

In 1971, American Indian students at Marquette University denounced the school nickname (Warriors) and mascot (Willie

Wampum, a white student dressed in buckskin regalia, wearing an oversized Indian-styled head) as degrading and demanded an immediate change. Their message, which appeared in the school newspaper, stated:

> The mascot is definitely offensive to the American Indian. We as native Americans have pride in our Indian heritage, and a mascot that portrays our forefathers' ancestral mode of dress for a laugh can be nothing but another form of racism. Having a non-Indian play the part is just as degrading to the Indian. From the past to contemporary times there is little the White man has not taken from the Indian. About the only thing left is our pride, and now Marquette University threatens to take that away from us by allowing such a display of racism. . . .We did not give our permission to be portrayed for a laugh, and we are sure no other minority group would condone such flagrant degradation of their heritage and pride. We ask that the mascot be discontinued completely. . . . We are sure the absence of the mascot would not take away any of the effectiveness of the Number 1 basketball team in the nation.[35]

Although the university eventually retired Willie Wampum and introduced a new nickname for its sports team (the Golden Eagles), the students' public statement is perhaps more important as a measure of the marked change in public opinion. Indian nicknames and symbols, long-accepted elements of sport, and embraced as a source of identity and entertainment have—after the cultural and political resurgence of Native America—become problematic, a source of contention, offense, and controversy. In the wake of the civil rights movement and at the height of the military conflict in Southeast Asia, a growing number of Americans began to recognize mascots as stereotypical, false, and hurtful images. Importantly, while other racist symbols like Frito Bandito or Sambo disappeared from American culture, a consensus about the meaning of Indian imagery in athletics did not take hold. As a result, over the past thirty-five years, Native American mascots have fostered intense conflicts about race, opportunity, and identity.

At sporting events, in public forums, in courtrooms, and in classrooms, individuals and institutions have challenged the continued use of Indian imagery in sports. Activists protesting may be the most visible sign of the controversy; of greater lasting significance, however, have been the countless political leaders, students, and everyday citizens who have openly expressed their concerns about Native American mascots. In response, political, religious, and professional organizations have taken a stand against such symbols. Groups who have spoken out against Native American mascots include the National Education Association, the United Church of Christ, the National Congress of American Indians, the Modern Language Association, the United Methodist Church, the American Anthropological Association, the Unitarian Universalist Association of Congregations, the United States Civil Rights Commission, and the American Indian Movement. Significantly, every major Native American organization with a national focus has voiced their opposition to Indian imagery in sports. Together, these public challenges have fostered heated discussions and policy reassessments in local communities and educational institutions across the country.

The past thirty-five years have witnessed remarkable changes. Many school boards, including the State Boards of Education of Minnesota and Nebraska and school districts in Los Angeles and Dallas, have passed resolutions requiring that schools change the Native American mascots. At the same time, some schools, such as the University of Utah, have altered their use of Indian imagery, while many others, such as Marquette University and Miami University (Ohio), have ended their use of such symbols altogether. In addition, litigation has proven important. Attorneys with the U.S. Department of Justice sought legal strategies to challenge mascots and remedy

In 2002, San Diego State University replaced its former mascot, Monty Montezuma, with Ambassador Montezuma (shown here). Anthropologists, historians, and community members offered their input on the new mascot's design and purpose.

their negative effects in court. Moreover, although overturned on appeal, the Trademark Trial and Appeal Board invalidated the Washington Redskins name in 2001 because it disparaged Native Americans and brought them "into contempt or disrepute." Finally, the media have taken a leading role in modifying public perceptions of mascots, as when the *Portland Oregonian* changed its editorial policy and refused to print derogatory team names.

Despite noteworthy advances, efforts to end the use of Indian imagery in athletics have met with opposition. Professional sports franchises have rejected calls for change. Consequently, prominent teams in baseball (Braves, Indians), hockey (Blackhawks), and football (Redskins) continue to profit from the stereotyping of indigenous peoples. And though educational institutions have been more responsive, many with Native American mascots have found ways to retain "their" Indians despite public concerns: some institutions have sought to find more authentic and appropriate ways of playing Indian at halftime. Marquette University, in the late 1970s, after retiring Willie Wampum, turned to the American Indian community on campus for a new mascot. The resulting First Warrior dressed in regalia and performed traditional dances. Negative response from fans and Native Americans in the region ultimately forced the university to select a non-Indian mascot. More recently, San Diego State University replaced Monty Montezuma with Ambassador Montezuma, a mascot designed in consultation with anthropologists, historians, and community members to be respectful and authentic. More commonly, educational institutions hold hearings and conduct surveys, as if discrimination and racism were a matter of opinion. In 2000, the University of Illinois undertook an elaborate investigation of its mascot, Chief Illiniwek, hiring a retired judge to preside over what it termed a "dialogue" that guaranteed opponents and supporters equal time. The final report sought a compromise that has yet to materialize. A year later, Glen Johnson, the president of Southeastern Oklahoma State University, which has long been known as the Savages, initiated a self-study, stating:

> I have asked the strategic planning council to determine if any change would be appropriate based on the school's long-term goal and mission. At this time we are under no deadline to make a decision. We want to proceed slowly to ensure that all points of view are heard.[36]

A consequence of such bureaucratic strategies is that they allow false and hurtful images of Native Americans to remain profitable and pleasurable, while refusing to engage the deleterious effects such imagery may have for indigenous peoples and the prospects of education and equality in the contemporary United States.

The Mascot Debate

Not surprisingly, the controversy over the continued use of Indian imagery in sports has fostered intense debate. At both the national and local levels, supporters and opponents of Native American mascots have formulated powerful arguments about what mascots mean and why they should be retained or retired. This section briefly summarizes the contrasting positions on American Indian nicknames and symbols, highlighting the underlying importance of each.

In Defense

Supporters of mascots offer a number of arguments designed to make such images acceptable and to defuse the controversy. They stress respect, intention, fairness, and commonsense notions of symbols, play, and politics.

To many who support mascots, the use of Indian imagery honors indigenous peoples. It pays tribute to their bravery, strength, independence, perseverance, and prowess. Consequently, the use of American Indian symbols and nicknames in sports is a compliment, rather than an insult, and hence supporters continue. In turn, Native Americans should be proud of the positive regard and prestigious recognition embodied by representations. Furthermore, supporters often couple arguments about honor with discussions of intentionality. Native American mascots, they insist, were never intended to hurt, defame, or belittle indigenous peoples. In his defense of Indian imagery at Florida State University, in 1993, then-President Dale W. Lick wedded these arguments skillfully:

> Recent critics have complained that the use of Indian symbolism is derogatory. Any symbol can be misused and become derogatory. This, however, has never been the intention at Florida State. Over the years we have worked closely with the Seminole tribe of Florida to ensure the dignity and propriety of the various symbols we use. . . . Some traditions

we cannot control. For instance, in the early 1980s, when our band, the Marching Chiefs, began the now famous arm motion while singing the "war chant," who knew that a few years later the gesture would be picked up by other teams' fans and named the "tomahawk chop?" It's a term we did not choose and officially do not use.[37]

Clearly, for Lick, and supporters more generally, if Native American mascots were not meant to be offensive or racist, to interpret them as such is unfair at best. Arguments in support of mascots, moreover, speak about race through analogies between Native Americans and other ethnic groups. Many supporters are proud to see "their heritage" displayed in an athletic context. It is not uncommon for someone with Scandinavian ancestry to declare their deep pride and satisfaction for the Minnesota Vikings or to hear others ask: Why isn't someone complaining about the Fighting Irish of Notre Dame? Unable to grasp the concerns voiced by opponents, defenders of mascots dismiss them as silly, examples of political correctness, and a diversion from other, more serious or genuine, problems demanding attention. They encourage detractors to "lighten up," "to get over it," "to grow up," "to get a life," "to get a grip," or "to get real." In part, this derives from a collective sense of sport as playful, set apart from everyday life. Moreover, this refusal to take mascots seriously arises from a common belief that symbols are unimportant—"it is just a name!" In a sense, supporters are suggesting both that it is all in fun and reiterating the accepted wisdom that while sticks and stones may break your bones, words can (or should) never hurt you.

Arguments in defense of mascots reveal a set of deeper assumptions as well. First, they refuse to engage or take seriously the concerns of living Native Americans in their defenses of "their" imagined Indians. Second, they exhibit a propensity to tell Native Americans how it is or how they should feel (namely respected and honored). Third, supporters display an inability and unwillingness to see or talk about race. When race does enter into their discussions, moreover, they qualify and constrain it. On the one hand, they suggest that racism is meaningful only when it is intentional, guided by ill-will, and truly significant (that is in the real world). On the other hand, many supporters claim parity between their ethnic heritage and racial condition and that of Native Americans, arguing that Irishness, for instance, is equivalent to Indianness in terms of the privileges, possibilities, and histories.

In Opposition

Opponents seek to undermine mascots and the arguments advanced in defense of them. Questioning supporters' familiarity with Native America and their knowledge of American history and society, opponents dispute assertions that mascots honor Native Americans. In particular, they highlight race, history, and power in their efforts to challenge the continued use of Indian nicknames and symbols.

Arguments against mascots pivot around race. Almost universally, opponents stress that Native American mascots are racist symbols that stereotype, demean, dehumanize, and injure indigenous peoples. Furthermore, some note with sadness that Americans embrace stereotypes of Native Americans that are no longer acceptable for other racial and ethnic groups. For instance, one cannot imagine a team called the Blackskins, but the professional football team in the nation's capitol is named the Redskins; one cannot reasonably conceive of an educational institution appropriating the religious artifacts or practices of Catholics or Jews and then using them for half-time entertainment as is presently done with objects sacred to indigenous peoples; and one has difficulty explaining why black face is problematic but playing Indian is not and why Frito Bandito was retired while Chief Wahoo continues to make money. These disparities, in turn, provoke others to actively strive to make the racial content of mascots tangible, linking them to a more palpable and familiar version of race. Commonly, opponents offer racial analogies, comparing Native Americans with other racial groups. Frequently, they invent new and intentionally provocative team names.[38]

In contrast with supporters, opponents of mascots stress history and power, situating nicknames and symbols in a broader context of oppression. They direct attention to the ways in which the continued use of Indian imagery in sports resonates with and derives from earlier, power-laden forms of disrespect and dehumanization, including stereotyping, forced removal, and assimilation. Others go so far as to link the history of American Indians with the Holocaust to emphasize the death and destruction at the heart of the American experience and underscore the disconnect between the historic mistreatment of indigenous peoples in the United States and the present desire to enshrine imaginary Indians as sport team mascots. Arresting the use of Indian imagery in sports, many opponents assert, would be an initial step to validating and respecting Native Americans.

Arguments advanced against Native American mascots turn on three key assumptions. First, they direct attention to racist images and their effects. Second, they actively racialize the debate over mascots, making analogies between the experience and condition of Native Americans and those of other racial groups, particularly African Americans. Third, they historicize the use of American Indian nicknames and symbols, connecting them with broader patterns of discrimination and oppression.

Significance of the Mascot Debate

Supporters and defenders of mascots clearly disagree about the significance of mascots. Whereas supporters insist that mascots foster respect and are meant to honor Native Americans, opponents assert that they denigrate Native Americans, perpetuating historical patterns of discrimination and dispossession. The distinct positions advanced in the unfolding debates point to deeper differences: Supporters stress text (honor, intention), while opponents emphasize context (history and racism). Supporters isolate; opponents make connections. Supporters argue for intent; opponents argue for effect. Supporters think of symbols and names as flat and more or less unimportant; opponents think of symbols as powerful cultural forms that reflect social relations and reinforce historical inequalities. Supporters deflect and deny the import of race; opponents highlight the centrality of race.

Indeed, they advance competing visions of race. Supporters, who might be described as advocates of a more-or-less dominant, if not reactionary, notion, hold that "we are all more or less equal," that the ill intentions of prejudiced individuals produce racism, and that discussions of discrimination should be confined to "real" and "important" social domains. In contrast, opponents advance a perspective that reads the social relations and cultural categories against the grain, exposing the power and meaning embedded within accepted norms, ideologies, and behaviors. They argue that race and racism are central to the American experience, that the effects of racial hierarchy cannot be ignored, and that symbols such as mascots—far from being frivolous—are significant measures of race relations. In this light, the ongoing controversy over mascots is as much about conflicting interpretations of race as it is a series of arguments over the appropriateness of Native American images in popular culture.

Mascots and Educational Institutions

Even if one accepts that the use of Indian imagery in sports derives from a sincere desire and well-intentioned effort to celebrate the ideals and consecrate the memory of indigenous peoples, such motives neither erase nor excuse the deleterious consequences often associated with Native American mascots. Such symbols diminish indigenous peoples. On the one hand, some have suggested that the uses of imaginary Indians in association with athletics contributes to the denigration of American Indian mental health. On the other hand, Native American mascots conspire with other negative stereotypes to deny indigenous peoples cultural citizenship, limiting their capacity to claim equality or exercise full personhood in everyday life. Sadly, educational institutions with Native American mascots provide clear and powerful testimony to the harmful effects associated with the continued use of Indian imagery in sports. To begin, such mascots miseducate. They teach students what American Indians are like; and because they rely on stereotypes and caricatures, they misconstrue the cultures and histories of Native nations. As a result, institutions charged with cultivating complex, humane, critical, and grounded understandings instead offer superficial, racist, normative, and fictional renderings. Moreover, because mascots encourage students, faculty, administrators, and the broader community not to recognize or understand American Indians for who they really are, they contribute to the continuing marginalization and exclusion of indigenous peoples. They cannot see actual Native Americans and hence exclude them from their institutional visions. It is not uncommon, for instance, for school board members to dismiss questions about a local mascot issue because the school district faces other, more pressing issues. Similarly, administrators at a predominantly Latino high school in Iowa have asserted that their mascot is not a problem because they do not have Indian students, overlooking the fact that a majority of their students from Latin America have Indian ancestry.[39]

The continued use of Native American mascots also has an adverse impact on curriculum. In a statement denouncing Chief Illiniwek, the University of Illinois Department of Anthropology succinctly summarized the way the mascot negatively affected its academic mission. Chief Illiniwek

(i) promotes inaccurate conceptions of the Native peoples

The debate rages at the University of Illinois over whether Chief Illiniwek (shown here on a banner) should remain the school's mascot. In 2000, the university undertook an elaborate investigation of its mascot, but the issue has yet to be resolved. In May 2005, the National Collegiate Athletic Association (NCAA) requested that thirty-one member institutions, including the University of Illinois, send reports detailing the primary reasons they support and oppose the use of their mascots.

of Illinois, past and present; (ii) undermines the effectiveness of our teaching and is deeply problematic for the academic environment both in and outside the classroom; (iii) creates a negative climate in our professional relationships with Native American communities that directly affects our ability to conduct research with and among Native American peoples; and, (iv) adversely affects the recruitment of Native American students and faculty into our university and department.[40]

The continued use of Indian imagery in athletics works against the ideals of educational institutions. It produces false knowledge, fosters hostility and discomfort, and undermines the creation of inclusive, democratic learning communities. Perhaps the most chilling examples of the hostile environments created by mascots emerge in the testimony of students of color (particularly, but not exclusively, Native American) at historically white colleges and universities with Native American mascots. They speak of how they feel silenced and misunderstood in the classroom, marginalized in the community, excluded from social life, and harassed by team boosters. Worse, Native American students often receive direct threats. Leaders in the movement to retire Chief Illiniwek in the late 1990s were subject to menacing phone calls, often describing physical harm, while boosters at the University of North Dakota posted handmade placards telling American Indian students to stop complaining, remember who won the war, and go back to the reservation where they belonged. Although condemned by administrators, such actions underscore the dehumanizing, undemocratic, and anti-Indian consequences that arise at schools with Native American mascots.

SUMMARY

Despite the established opposition of American Indian leaders, harmful effects, and ongoing controversy, educational institutions and sports teams likely will retain Native American mascots for the foreseeable future. Indeed, there are at least six reasons such nicknames and symbols will remain prominent for some time to come. First, there is not a shared understanding about what it means to use Indian imagery. In fact, most Americans have limited appreciation of the history of stereotyping and racism and why they still matter today. Second, the ongoing debate is not, as suggested above, a dialogue, but a cultural battle between entrenched positions. Third, almost invariably, individuals and institutions have fashioned elaborate traditions that make mascots powerful as ways to know oneself, recall the past, have fun, and bond with others. Fourth, the demands placed on colleges and universities—to please alumni, to attract donors, to recruit students, to value diversity, to teach critical thinking, and to market themselves as a distinct brand—make it difficult for them to do the morally right thing. Fifth, Native American mascots are profitable, well-known names and symbols that continue to be marketed to eager fans, and hence remain lucrative for teams and schools. Sixth, as long as movies and journalism, not to mention educational institutions themselves, continue to shape public opinion about American Indians through partial, superficial, inaccurate, and even stereotypical accounts of indigenous peoples, Native American mascots will thrive.

5

Indigenous Media

The preceding chapters raise a question asked too infrequently: How might the stories and images central to mainstream media be different if they incorporated American Indian perspectives? A recent study by Elizabeth Bird provides a partial answer to this query. Bird, an anthropologist interested in what authors and audiences make of media images, brought together small focus groups of Euro-Americans and Native Americans, asking them to design a television program featuring at least three characters, a woman, a white, and an American Indian. Although all of the groups referenced popular shows and suggested familiar storylines in the creative process, they displayed important differences in how they perceived Indians and Indianness.[41]

White participants drew upon the Hollywood Indian, as found in *Pocahontas* and *Northern Exposure*. Moreover, they tended to render the proposed Native American characters through stereotypes, including names thought to sound Indian (Morning Star, Blackhawk, Redbird, and Sunbear), attributes commonly associated with American Indians (earthiness, spirituality, and even alcoholism), and settings that immediately bring to mind Native Americans (tribal-run casinos). Importantly, the shows developed by the Euro-American focus groups reflected their own lives and the preoccupations of the mainstream media, rather than actualities and complexities of American Indian life. As a consequence, white participants often had no idea how to flesh out Native American characters, and when they did, the roles tended to be less developed and more ancillary. Oddly, despite the pronounced presence of American Indians in the region where Bird conducted the study, they were not visible to the Euro-American focus groups.

In contrast, the Native American focus groups had a keen understanding of white society and its distorted and hurtful interpretations of them. In fact, the American Indian participants used the proposed shows to correct and counter dominant misunderstandings, while offering empowering alternatives. In addition, the pilots they drafted reflected on Indian/white relations, including colonialism and racism, their exclusion from history, what it means to be Indian, and the importance of affirming cultural heritage. Unlike their Euro-American counterparts, the Native American participants were not limited by the media or their world of experience, nor did they simply recycle stereotypes; instead, they actively engaged media images, proposing alternatives that used the format of the television show to challenge mainstream assumptions and to validate Indianness.

These differences underscore a fundamental truth: If Native Americans controlled the means of media production, both the content and form would be very different. Unfortunately, Native Americans do not at present control a large portion of the media. In the late 1990s, there were 11,577 radio stations, 1,518 television stations, 11,385 cable stations, and 1,456 low-power television operations in the United States. Of these, Americans Indians owned twenty-five radio stations and a half dozen low-power television operations. These numbers speak volumes about the limitations of indigenous access, authority, and influence in contemporary radio and television. At the same time, much like the standard histories of mainstream media outlined in preceding chapters, they conceal the vibrancy of indigenous media. Native Americans have actively participated in mainstream media, and more importantly have struggled for more than 150 years to establish alternative media—rooted in Native traditions and tribal communities—that would more accurately and authentically render their experience, and challenge inequalities and misunderstandings, while also reclaiming heritage and identity.

This chapter outlines the unique history and deep significance of indigenous media, specifically focusing on journalism and film. Whereas the American Indian press reminds us that indigenous media is nothing new, Native American film highlights a renaissance in Indian Country. These media share in common a capacity to empower, educate, affirm, and oppose, and consequently, contribute to ongoing efforts to reassert cultural sovereignty.

AMERICAN INDIAN PRESS

Despite the biases and barriers of the mainstream media, Native Americans have actively contributed to journalism as reporters, editors, and owners for more than 175 years. Sadly, these individuals are too often forgotten. Following Indian Removal, in the 1830s, Cherokee Elias C. Boudinot edited the *Arkansian* in Fayetteville. Two decades later, in 1856, John Rollin Ridge and Charles Waite, both Cherokees, were editors of the California paper *American*. The following year, John Ridge served as the founding editor of the *Sacramento Bee*, later owning and editing several other California papers. Near the turn of the twentieth century, Myrta Eddleman (Cherokee) became the sole owner of the *Muskogee* (OK) *Daily Times,* Edward Bushyhead (Cherokee) founded the *San Diego Union,* and Peter Navarre (Potawatomi) owned the *Rossville* (KS) *Reporter.* American Indian journalists were to be found on the radio shortly after its invention as well. For instance, from 1924 to 1932, Ora Eddleman Reed (Cherokee), known as the Sunshine Lady, hosted one of the first "talk-type" shows on KDFN in Casper, Wyoming. And more recently, Native American journalists, including Hattie Kauffman and Tanna Beebe have made an impact on television reporting as well.[42]

Despite the trailblazing efforts of these and many other indigenous journalists, the mainstream press has largely failed to fairly report on Native American issues or to adequately incorporate American Indian voices and perspectives in its coverage. Or in the words of Rose W. Robinson, "The general media never covered Indian affairs except when it was about crime, tragedy, or a stereotypical event or activity. They never had any interest in providing news to Indian listeners or addressing misconceptions. Seeing the world through other eyes all the time can be frustrating and anger provoking."[43]

Today, one can find an array of newspapers from throughout Indian Country that are born of such frustrations and intent to rewrite the past, present, and future so that they include indigenous voices. There are dailies with a national profile, such as *Indian Country Today* or *Native American News,* that speak to pan-Indian and non-Indian audiences. At a regional level, newspapers like *Native Nevadan* (founded in 1964) and *Talk Leaf* (founded in Los Angeles in 1935) strive to keep diverse audiences informed about current events. Still more numerous are tribal newspapers, including the *Navajo Times* and *Yakama Nation Review,* which often serve as the official newspaper for Native nations. Similarly, intertribal newspapers have readers from more than one tribe. For instance, *Char-koosta* (published briefly in 1954 and revived in 1962), in Dixon, Montana, is the major source of news for the Salish,

Current Events, or *Adahooniligii*, was a monthly newsletter distributed to the Navajo Reservation in the 1940s. The newsletter used the Harrington-LaFarge alphabet, which was developed by Smithsonian Institution employees Oliver LaFarge and John P. Harrington in the 1930s. Today, the *Navajo Times* serves as the Navajo Nation's official newspaper.

Pen d'Oreilles, and Kootenais. For all of this diversity of scale, funding, and audience, the American Indian press shares a proud heritage and a common set of obstacles.

Native American journalism began in February 1828, when Elias Boudinot founded the *Cherokee Phoenix*, which has the distinction of being the first Indian-owned newspaper and the first newspaper published in a Native American language (though some stories were published in English as well). Boudinot used his paper to foster empowerment, education, and arguably assimilation. Beginning in 1829, when it changed its name to *Cherokee Phoenix and Indian Advocate*, the paper became explicitly political, intervening in the ongoing push to remove the Cherokees from their homelands to the newly created Indian Territory. Six years after it began, the groundbreaking paper ceased publication.

Shortly after removal, the Cherokee Nation began printing an official paper, the *Cherokee Advocate* (1843–1853). Bilingual, it sought to speak to both Cherokee and Euro-American readers alike. It also sought to empower and educate. In the words of founding editor and Princeton graduate William P. Ross:

> The object of the [Cherokee National] Council in providing for the publication of the *Advocate* is the physical, moral, and intellectual improvement of the Cherokee people. It will be devoted to these ends, and to the defense of those rights recognized as belonging to them in treaties legally made at different times with the United States, and of such measures as seem best calculated to secure their peace and happiness, promote their prosperity, and elevate their character as a distinct community.[44]

The guiding principles of progressivism, sovereignty, and community were expressed more plainly in the paper's motto: "Our Right. Our Country. Our Race."

Indigenous journalism also flourished among other Native nations forcibly removed from the East. The short-lived *Intelligencer*, a contemporary of the *Cherokee Advocate*, was published in Doaksville, Oklahoma, then capital of the Choctaw Nation. It was bilingual, carrying general news, obituaries, accounts of legal proceedings, and the weather. Under the slogan, "Universal Love and Charity Our Shield: Our Only

Weapon Truth," the *Intelligencer*, much like its progressive contemporaries, had high aspirations. The editors avowed:

> The paper is designed to be an advocate of genuine morality, sound education, and Temperance, and a source of information in regard to agriculture and the markets ... [as well as] history, Indian traditions, manners, and customs, and to such other subjects as may be suitable in a Family newspaper.[45]

The *Intelligencer* was much more than a source of information. It charged itself with a unique mission: communicating about history, heritage, and Indianness. Less political than other papers in Indian Country, it was no less aware of its special role.

In many respects, the commitment to educate and empower remains central to the American Indian press. It echoes in the establishment of the American Indian Press Association (founded in 1971, renamed the Native American Journalists Association [NAJA] in 1984), an intertribal group open to all intent to communicate news to Indian Country, train future journalists through internships and scholarship programs, and bring an indigenous perspective to the world of journalism. Moreover, the spirit that invigorated nineteenth-century indigenous newspapers also animated *A'tome*, a newspaper published by the Northern Cheyennes in Montana. The biweekly sought to address the threats posed by mining interests, enhance the commercial climate on the reservation, establish job training, and improve communication, while promoting "in all ways the retaining of tribal cultural values . . . strengthen[ing] the human individualism inherent in such traditionally stable social systems."[46] To these ambitious ends, the editor added: "Improving the future lot of Indian people by interceding and promoting greater understanding and sympathy among the general public." Again, journalism is more than a set of stories, a means to communicate the truth, or a way to make money. For its nearly two-hundred-year history, the American Indian press has endeavored to preserve cultural heritage, empower its Indian readers, intervene in broader social and political struggles, and educate its non-Indian audience.

Clearly, indigenous newspapers differed markedly from those owned and edited by Euro-Americans. Nowhere was this difference starker than in the attitudes expressed about the so-called Indian wars. The mainstream (white) press celebrated, justified, and at times incited violence perpetuated by settlers and soldiers. In contrast, the American Indian press advocated racial solidarity, defended indigenous cultures, and remained vigilant about the actions of outsiders. In March 1876, three months before the Battle of the Little Bighorn, the *Cherokee Advocate* published a powerful commentary on the state of race relations by invoking the memory of Custer's 1868 attack on Cheyenne chief Black Kettle's village:

> The Inhabitants were peacefully and harmlessly asleep . . . Custer drew his troops about the defenceless village, and everything disposed, a loud shout was raised and drums beaten. The Indians came rushing out in alarm, and as they appeared the troops poured in volley and volley and shot them all down. Sheridan then telegraphed, "A glorious victory."[47]

The attack is here rendered a massacre, an inhuman act that Euro-Americans celebrate as a joyous event. In publishing this editorial, and then again later after the defeat of Custer's command, the *Advocate* and its peers in Indian Country often reprinted letters and commentaries from white authors, originally published in the mainstream press. Such a tactic was obviously meant to deflect criticism and protect the paper, if not its readers. It suggests, moreover, that the anti-Indian hostility of the day, which encouraged near genocidal campaigns against the Lakotas and others, also hemmed in the American Indian press.

Even when Native American journalists spoke against white power, their terms were measured, their tone reserved. Consider for example what William P. Boudinot, editor of the *Cherokee Advocate,* wrote of Custer's fate in July 1876:

> Undoubtedly the plan of General Custer was a good one if the Indians he was to fight had been the same class as the Indians he had been accustomed to fight before . . . But unfortunately, for him they were not of that class. He made the mistake so often made of confounding all Indians alike. The mistake cost him his life if not his reputation.[48]

Boudinot clearly condemns Custer and anti-Indian racism simultaneously, but he does not celebrate the defeat, critique the policy of the federal government, or valorize the Lakotas and Cheyennes who fended off Custer. And it is perhaps here as well that the power and possibility, no less than the limitations and marginality, of the American Indian press becomes most palpable.

Although virulent anti-Indian racism no longer limits the Native American press as it did in 1876, its promise has yet to be fully realized. Indeed, despite the establishment of organizations like NAJA, technological advances, and increasing numbers of professional journalists, the Native American press faces a number of obstacles. In contrast to the mainstream media, Native American newspapers often lack adequate funding. As a consequence, they must deal with problems associated with unreliable and unpredictable scheduling, staffing, and formatting. Making matters worse, the American Indian press frequently must endure cultural and geographic isolation. Moreover, despite great progress over the past quarter century, newspapers in Indian Country still display less objectivity and hire more inexperienced staffs. Finally, although they should enjoy constitutional protections, American Indian reporters and editors are often not safeguarded by First Amendment protections. In large measure, tribal ownership creates situations in which they cannot fully or freely express themselves. For all of these impediments, the American Indian press continues to thrive, dedicated throughout to empowering and educating as it defends heritage and sovereignty.

NATIVE AMERICAN FILM

If the American Indian press emerged both as a defensive response to assimilation and removal and a progressive movement to affirm Indianness, Native American film was born as part of a larger renaissance intent on reclaiming cultural and political sovereignty. A series of social movements and policy initiatives in the 1960s provided the foundation for the materialization of indigenous cinema, including the civil rights movement, decolonization struggles in the Third World, protests against the Vietnam War, the solidification of youth culture, the explosion of Red power, and the war on poverty. At the same time, the Bureau of Indian Affairs established the Institute of American Indian Arts (IAIA) in 1962. AIAI proposed that "traditional expressions in the arts by American Indians can be extended . . . [and] enriched in its present state by techniques that will consider the universal forces of creativity, contemporary demands, and respect for cultural difference."[49] Simultaneously, anthropologist Sol Worth undertook a study of how Navajo youth used video media and how Hollywood insiders sought to open doors to minorities, including Native Americans.

Of equal importance, American Indians, often in collaboration with existing mainstream media organizations, have fashioned an increasingly sophisticated infrastructure, promoting creative and critical work. Arguably, the most important development for filmmaking in Indian Country was the establishment of the Native American Public Broadcasting Consortium in 1977, later renamed Native American Public Telecommunications (NAPT) in 1995. Receiving funding primarily from the Corporation for Public Broadcasting, NAPT has striven to become "the authoritative national resource for authentic, culturally educational, and entertaining programming by and about Native Americans."[50]

To achieve this objective, NAPT has collaborated with tribal communities, encouraged the production of high-quality cinematic work by indigenous writers, directors, and producers, and reached out to audiences across Native America. During the past decade, NAPT has matured, undertaking ambitious projects to enhance the visibility and availability of Native American film. It joined the American Indian Higher Education Consortium, creating a satellite network among tribal colleges. At the same time, it sponsored five documentary series broadcast on public television in the 1990s. Perhaps its most significant initiative was the creation of Visionmaker Video, a production company that seeks, according to its motto, to empower, educate, and entertain.

While organizations like NAPT have provided much-needed infrastructure, educational institutions and industry-sponsored seminars have given aspiring filmmakers the requisite skills to realize their creative visions. For example, in the late 1960s and early 1970s, the American Film Institute and Anthropology Film Center offered workshops in Santa Fe, New Mexico, training filmmakers and artists like Milo Yellow Hair (cowriter and narrator of the acclaimed documentary *In the Spirit of Crazy Horse*), Joy Harjo, Gloria Bird, and George Burdeau (first Native American member of the Director's Guild of America and director of *Backbone of the World: The Blackfeet*). More recently, Montana State University launched the Native Voices Public Television Workshop in 1990, producing important films by talented American Indian filmmakers, such as Roy Bigcrane, who directed the historical documentary *The Place of Falling Waters*, and Terry Macy's moving biography of a quadriplegic Blackfeet artist—*Ernie Peppion: The Human Touch*. Educational institutions, such as the Center for Media, Culture, and History at New York University, have also established fellowships for indigenous filmmakers, granting them time and money to pursue their creative work.

Although film festivals have become a chic venue for art house and independent cinema, those devoted to creative work by American Indian writers and directors have proven crucial to the growth and success of Native American film. Importantly, such events not only give these films much-deserved visibility and publicity, they also reiterate the uniqueness of indigenous media, particularly its commitment to education, empowerment, heritage, and identity. The vision statement of the 1991 Two Rivers Native American Film and Video Festival in Minneapolis encapsulates the key cultural commitments of American Indian cinema:

> The vision was to bring to our community a Native film and video festival that honors the richness of our cultures while celebrating the strength of the native spirit. As we began to organize we found many creative people who were honoring this spirit. We spoke with them and learned of their work, it became apparent that the messages and stories they were telling were that all people need to hear. Their stories reveal the endurance of our cultures and our connections to our earth mother . . . these new storytellers and visionaries of our people . . . are using their gifts to describe in our own words and images who we are as Native people. They are helping us to reclaim our identities while challenging others to rethink their perceptions of us.[51]

In addition to numerous local and regional film screenings by Native Americans, both the American Indian Film Institute in San Francisco and the National Museum of the American Indian (New York Branch) sponsor internationally renowned film festivals.

Together, these institutions and initiatives have laid the foundation for the emergence of a vibrant, culturally literate, and politically engaged American Indian cinema. Documentaries

Chris Eyre (Cheyenne-Arapaho), a native of Klamath Falls, Oregon, directed the 1998 movie *Smoke Signals*, which tells the story of two teenage Native Americans (Thomas and Victor) who live on a reservation in Idaho and set out on a road trip to collect the ashes of Victor's estranged father.

dominate Native American film and video production; very few features have been made by American Indians, most notably *Smoke Signals*, written by Sherman Alexie (Spokane-Coeur d'Alene) and directed by Chris Eyre (Cheyenne-Arapaho), and *Skins*, directed by Eyre. In part, material conditions and the mechanics of filmmaking have encouraged Native American directors to turn to the documentary format: it is cheaper and more flexible, requiring a smaller crew and less-established distribution network. Of equal, if not greater, significance, the film industry continues to exclude indigenous perspectives and personnel. Indeed, in response to the dour prediction of Michael Apted (the Euro-American director of *Thunderheart*) that an American Indian would never direct a Hollywood feature, Native American filmmaker Sandra Osawa remarked, "Well, it's not the infrastructure . . . I believe it has something to do with racism."[52] Significantly, in spite of barriers in mainstream media, Native Americans have produced hundreds of powerful, moving, and important films.

Native American Cinematic Themes

Countless Native American films seek to unsettle common-sense understandings and accepted stereotypes of indigenous cultures and histories. Some, like *Imagining Indians* by Hopi director Victor Masayesva, Jr., directly confront the Hollywood Indian, reflecting on the consequences of such distortions for Native peoples and communities. Others, such as *Smoke Signals*, subtly demolish preconceptions, first by portraying a range of American Indian characters, all of which challenge prevailing ideas about Indianness, and second, by using humor to expose how anti-Indian images confine and crush them. They figuratively, as indicated in the title of Beverly Singer's book, "wipe the war paint off the lens."

American Indian cinema routinely documents people and practices meaningful to Native Americans. Both *On and off the Reservation with Charlie Hill*, a biographical portrait of the beloved Oneida Comedian by Sandra Osawa, and *I'd Rather Be Powwowing*, a documentary produced by George Horse Capture (Gros Ventre) and directed by Larry Littlebird (Laguna-Santo Domingo), exemplify this element of contemporary indigenous visual media. At the same time, this theme is not exclusively happy and celebratory. In fact, it routinely probes difficult political issues and social problems facing Native American communities. *Skins*, for instance, grapples with life on the Pine Ridge Reservation, alcoholism, and sibling relations; and, Mona Smith's *Her Giveaway* (like several other of her films) confronts HIV/AIDS in Indian Country.

Native American films frequently make sense of the present by retelling histories. Such films and videos draw upon indigenous storytelling practices and incorporate indigenous perspectives on the past. The award-winning *Surviving Columbus: The Story of the Pueblo People*, directed by Diane Reyna (Taos/San Juan Pueblo) and produced by George Burdeau, typifies this feature of Native American cinema, as it speaks against celebratory praise for Columbus and Western civilization generally, offering instead a tale of Pueblo resistance to colonialism and survival of repeated efforts to assimilate them.

Many American Indian filmmakers, much like their peers throughout Indian Country, have displayed an interest in reclaiming sovereignty and affirming heritage. Many films detail struggles to assert treaty rights or exercise constitutionally guaranteed freedoms. Sandra Osawa's *Lighting the 7th Fire*, which explores Ojibwa fishing rights in Wisconsin, exemplifies the former, while Ava Hamilton's (Arapaho-Cheyenne) study of federal curtailment of American Indian religious freedom, *Everything Has a Spirit*, represents the latter. Equally important, indigenous video media records and respects cultural traditions. To speak only of dance, examples range from the aforementioned documentary on powwow to Phil Lucas' (Choctaw) and Hanay Geiogamah's (Kiowa) *Dances for the New Generation*.

Native American cinema almost invariably contemplates, reflects upon, and struggles with Indianness, questioning competing interpretations of Native identity. They ask in both simple and complex, blatant and subtle ways: What does it mean to be an American Indian? This question haunts movies as diverse as Sherman Alexie's *The Business of Fancydancing*, Lumbee filmmaker Malinda Maynor's *Real Indians*, and Arlene Bowman's (Diné) *Navajo Talking Picture*.

Since *Smoke Signals*

In the wake of *Smoke Signals*, indigenous filmmakers have made a steady stream of features. Three recent films deserve special mention: *The Business of Fancydancing, Skins,* and *Fast Runner*.

Sherman Alexie wrote and directed *The Business of Fancydancing*, the semi-autobiographical story of Indian poet Seymour Polatkin. Combining flashbacks, dance, poetry readings, and dramatic dialogue, it wrestles with unexpected issues, including the tensions between city and reservation, the costs of success, resentment, and identity. Refusing to reduce its characters to superficial traits (such as sexuality—Polatkin is gay), it renders them in complex and current terms that make it impossible to return to dated stereotypes so common in mainstream cinema.

In *Skins*, Chris Eyre, who directed *Smoke Signals*, renders a wrenching portrait of contemporary Native life. Set on the Pine Ridge Reservation in South Dakota, the film tells the story of two brothers, one a police officer, the other an alcoholic. It traces the hardship of reservation life, the lasting impact of history, and the tragic consequences of anger and injury. Although criticized for offering an overly negative vision, *Skins* nicely captures the complexities of struggle and survival too often hidden from view.

Fast Runner, the first film in the Inuktitut language, won the Camera d'Or at the Cannes Film Festival, was nominated for an Oscar, and became a surprise box office success. It retells a traditional Inuit tale that is both melodramatic and tragic. The nearly three-hour-long movie takes up universal human themes, including star-crossed love, jealousy, and betrayal. The beautiful cinematography and storytelling, combined with its rendering of the natural scenery and small communal setting, showcase the unique power of traditional tales and Native perspectives for Western audiences.

These three films underscore the promise of indigenous media. They emphasize the vitality of Native American artists, while suggesting the potential for future features.

Finally, as they speak to indigenous audiences and retell their histories, challenge stereotypes, affirm sovereignty, and wrestle with identity, Native American films educate a broader public. In the process, they open intercultural dialogues that hold the promise of altering how non-Indians interpret and engage with indigenous cultures and histories.

Whether feature films or documentaries, Native American film is arguably on the cutting edge of contemporary indigenous media in North America. Often humorous, regularly critical, and always reflecting and corroborating American Indian traditions and sensibilities, documentaries and features by, for, and about Native Americans strive to uplift, instruct, and reclaim identity, history, culture, and sovereignty.

SUMMARY

Although too easily forgotten, indigenous media has for nearly two hundred years struggled to empower Native Americans and educate the general public. American Indian journalism and cinema have proven crucial to the negotiation of identity, heritage, and sovereignty. Where the mainstream media, federal policy, and a majority of Americans have long diagnosed, measured, and lamented "the Indian problem," indigenous media have proposed Indian solutions. Having paired a sound infrastructure with creative talent, the future of American Indian newspapers and films are bright, even far beyond Indian Country. In 2001, Beverly Singer expressed with pride and joy:

> Watching Smoke Signals (1998) at a West Hollywood theater in the summer of 1998 was a new movie-going experience for me. I went to see the film because it was written by Sherman Alexie (Spokane/Coeur d'Alene) and directed by Chris Eyre (Cheyenne/Arapaho). I am ready to see more films made by my people. I hope another century won't go by before we get to enjoy at a local theater another film by Native people.[53]

I, too, trust that indigenous productions and perspectives increasingly will cross over, entering the mainstream media as legitimate, important elements of an intercultural dialogue about tradition, community, and the future.

6

The Internet and the Future of Native Americans in the Media

In 2000, Myra Jodie won a new iMac. Although surely a stroke of good luck, this event is more instructive for what it says about the promise and problem of new media for Native Americans. Apple had difficulty contacting the Navajo (Diné) teenager and was forced to notify her at high school, because she, like many in her home community, had no telephone. Ironically, the computer company had sought to promote the ease of connecting to the Internet, but by awarding it to a young woman in a community where some live ten or more miles from the nearest pay phone and only the smallest fraction have a computer, let alone Internet access, Apple instead demonstrated the continuing marginalization of Native Americans and the obstacles that may prevent them from realizing the potential of this new media.[54]

In this chapter, direct attention is paid to Indians on the Internet. The primary focus is on Web sites owned and operated by Native individuals, organizations, and nations. In the process, Native American access to the Web is detailed, which underscores the barriers that have prevented them from participating equally in cyber culture, as well as their presence online, highlighting the diversity of Web sites run by and for indigenous peoples and influences on site design. Against this background, ongoing debates within Indian Country over the social implications of the Web are considered. The chapter closes with a set of guidelines for assessing Web sites.

BARRIERS TO WEB USE

In many respects, the World Wide Web remains overwhelming for white, male, urban, and middle, if not upper, class people. Few Native Americans use the Internet, largely because they do not have the resources necessary to get online. Telephone ownership hints at how limited access is in Indian Country. Whereas 95 percent of Americans have telephones, the number of Indians with phones is far lower. On the Navajo Reservation, for instance, less than 40 percent do. With these figures in mind, it is not surprising that only 15 percent of Native Americans have computers and approximately 10 percent of Native Americans have Internet access. Another way to measure the constrained participation of indigenous peoples online is to consider the number of tribes with Web pages. At the start of the twenty-first century, there are more than 550 federally recognized tribes in the United States, but only 132 of them (or less than 25 percent) have Web sites.[55]

There are several features of contemporary Native American life that make it difficult, if not impossible, for many Native Americans to access the Internet. First, more than one quarter of Native Americans live below the poverty line. Consequently, many American Indians lack the economic resources necessary to get online. Second, a large plurality of American Indians live in rural areas, underserved, if not completely unserved, by multinational media conglomerates who do not wire rural America because they cannot turn a profit. Third, levels of educational attainment hamper Internet access. Indeed, nationwide, 25 percent of American Indians drop out of high school. And in some states the number is much higher. In Montana, for instance, more than 50 percent of Native American students drop out before graduating. Finally, because of their rural location, historical underdevelopment, impoverishment, and the presence of more pressing needs, many reservations lack the technological infrastructure needed to connect residents to the World Wide Web.

In addition to these structural barriers, popular ideas about Native Americans pose a fundamental, if an often overlooked, hindrance. Indeed, existing media and the images they have created make it impossible for indigenous peoples' full participation in cyberspace. Not surprisingly, the stereotypes discussed in previous chapters populate the World Wide Web. One cannot only encounter Chief Wahoo or Chief Illiniwek repeatedly when bouncing around pages devoted to sports but read pages meant to sanction such false and hurtful imagery. Image searches for "Indian Princess" (or similar variation) at Google is more likely to retrieve a still from Disney's *Pocahontas*, a scantily clad white woman in headdress for Halloween, or nineteenth-century product logo than to find a picture of an American Indian woman that is realistic and respectful. And, one can with little difficulty find any number of Web sites rooted in the tradition of playing Indian, from Web pages for youth groups, like Y-Indian Princess and scouting troops, to New Age Web sites by shamans peddling (what they claim is) Native spirituality to an eager and alienated public. Worse are the numerous anti-Indian sites on the Internet, intent on undermining the sovereignty of Native nations, take away treaty rights, or profit from indigenous cultures and histories. As long as American Indians are not seen as human and not accorded equal access, they will be unable to fully participate in cyberculture, and in turn, the World Wide Web can never realize its promise.

SCOPE OF WEB USE

Despite these barriers, Native individuals and organizations increasingly have seized upon the Internet to make connections, educate themselves and others, influence policy, enhance cultural preservation, and communicate who they are within a broader world. Lisa Mitten, who maintains a Web page compiling links to indigenous Web sites (*http://www.nativecul-turelinks.com/indians.html*), summarizes the growth and development of the Indian presence online.[56] Soon after its inception in 1995, she listed a total of 33 Web pages. Eight years later, she had 192 links divided into 11 categories. Further evidence of this trend can be found in the recent designation of *nsn.us* (Native sovereign nation in the United States) as an exclusive suffix for tribal Web addresses.

In a recent review article, Mitten identifies eight distinct kinds of Native American Web sites. First, *mega-sites*, arguably the most useful type of site, have proven among the most difficult to maintain. Mega-sites collect together links of numerous other Web sites, serving as a "clearing house" of knowledge, which make excellent resources. In addition to Mitten's own Web site, other examples of mega-sites include Nativeweb (*http://www.nativeweb.org*) and the Virtual Library run by Karen Strom (*http://www.hanksville.org/Naresources*). Second, as mentioned previously, 132 of the federally recognized tribes currently have Web pages. Mitten dubs these *tribal Web sites*. Importantly, she notes, many of these oldest and prominent examples within this category are associated with tribes that have large populations, such as the Cherokee and the Iroquois. Third, local, regional, national, and international *Native American organizations* have a pronounced presence online, ranging from National Congress for American Indians (*http://www.ncai.org*) and the Native American Sports Council (*http://nascsports.org*) to the Intertribal Bison Cooperative (*http://www.intertribalbison.org*) and the American Indian Center of Chicago (*http://www.aic-chicago.org*). Fourth, *education Web sites* include tribal colleges and other schools serving American Indians; national and regional organizations, like the American Indian Higher Education Consortium (*http://www.aihec.org*); alumni groups; and homepages for specific pedagogic projects. Fifth, a whole cluster of Web sites focus on *language*, including sites devoted to language preservation programs affiliated with tribes (*http://www.comanchelanguage.org*) and universities (*http://www.uaf.edu/anlc*), and organizations dedicated to teaching Native languages, such as Society for the Study of the Indigenous Languages of the Americas (*http://www.ssila.org*). Sixth, the World Wide Web has become important to the promotion and distribution of *indigenous media*. Examples include newspapers, such as *Indian Country Today* (*http://www.indiancountry.com*) and *Native American Times* (*http://www.nativetimes.com*), media groups, such as Native American Public Telecommunications (*http://www.nativetele-com.org*) and the American Journalist Association (*http://www.naja.com*), and online radio stations, including American Indian Radio on Satellite (*http://www.airos.org*). Seventh, similarly, the Internet has become home to countless *music Web sites*, ranging from homepages for recording companies to musical artists and groups. Eight, *business Web sites* constitute a final category, including small businesses, artists and craftspeople, and independent consultants.

Native American Web sites vary from premium quality and technologically sophisticated to plain and rudimentary. A number of factors influence design. First, the anticipated audience shapes the content, mode of address, and technology use. Language offers a good illustration of this pattern. A Web site designed for tourists, as opposed to tribal members would almost certainly be in English primarily. In contrast, sites designed for tribal members, frequently incorporate indigenous languages. The homepage of the Mohawk tribe in Canada, for instance, is written in Mohawk. And, on the Oklahoma Cherokee Web site, not only are the navigation buttons in

Cherokee, but the site features a Cherokee "word of the day." Second, financial resources play an important role, limiting both the kind and quality of Web site produced. Third, technological infrastructure on many reservation communities is underdeveloped, which again constrains the types of Web sites created.

To further illuminate the differences between tribal Web sites, Ellen L. Arnold and Darcy C. Plymire recently compared the homepage of the Cherokee Nation of Oklahoma (*http://www.cherokee.org*) and the Eastern Band of Cherokee in North Carolina (*http://Cherokee-nc.com*).[57] Whereas the Cherokee Nation is quite large, with constituents concentrated in Oklahoma and across the country, the Eastern Band is relatively small in size, primarily located in and around the Great Smoky Mountains in North Carolina. The former uses its Web site to provide information about community events, governmental services, tribal history, and traditional culture; the latter, in contrast, highlights cultural history and diversions, as well as recreation for tourists visiting western North Carolina or the Blue Ridge Parkway. The Cherokee Nation writes about services and society to cultural insiders (tribal members), while the Eastern Band writes about sightseeing and society with cultural outsiders (tourists). These choices reflect community size, economic opportunity, if not necessity, divergent histories, and distinct users of their Web sites.

Among the more interesting suggestions in the research conducted by Arnold and Plymire is that online Native Americans have appropriated a mainstream technology and used it for their own ends, including economic success and cultural preservation. This is a common phenomenon. The Internet has become increasingly important to the efforts of indigenous peoples to communicate about themselves with a broader audience, fostering efforts to rename themselves and reclaim their pasts. It has played a prominent role in ongoing efforts to preserve and revitalize culture, language, and tradition, and in the process has contributed to the reassertion of American Indian identities locally and nationally. In addition to its economic utility and cultural value, the Internet allows individuals and organizations to become more politically active as well. On the one hand, a number of Web sites seek to call attention to and even challenge

Online Activism

Although there are clear limitations, including technological access, the Internet promises to be important for American Indian politics. It affords tribes an opportunity to reach their members and to speak to a broader public. It encourages individuals and organizations to direct attention to issues affecting indigenous peoples, while giving voice to perspectives rarely heard in the mainstream media. Consequently, the World Wide Web has re-energized American Indian activism, offering a new medium and novel means to fight anti-Indian racism and media misrepresentations.

Reaction to the Outkast performance at the 2004 Grammy Awards provides a perfect example of the emerging political uses of the Internet. As described at the beginning of chapter 3, the popular hip-hop group dressed in outlandish attire and enacted a series of clichés associated with American Indians. Many Native Americans watching the performance were outraged, taking offense at the appropriation and trivialization of indigenous cultures. Making matters worse, a national television network implicitly endorsed the act and the mainstream media was all but silent about the event. Almost immediately, individuals critiqued the performance on music industry and Native Web sites. They opened debate about the imagery and sought to educate fans. At the same time, others pushed for collective action. They used electronic forums to initiate letter-writing campaigns and petitions intent to garner an apology and prevent future harm. Importantly, the online organizing translated into real-world action as well: On the one hand, it led some to boycott Outkast, their record label (Arista), and/or CBS; on the other hand, it helped to build a coalition directed at broader change.

The Internet undoubtedly will continue to serve as a vehicle for political protest in Indian Country, alerting mainstream society to the importance of understanding indigenous cultures and histories.

anti-Indian racism; on the other hand, the Internet has also forged novel connections among activists and promoted innovative interventions. For instance, the World Wide Web has proved crucial to efforts in California to prohibit the use of American Indian imagery in athletics and to a petition drive against the performance by Outkast at the Grammys.

PROMISE OR PROBLEM?

Although unnoticed by most of the mainstream media, Native Americans have argued over the social implications of the World Wide Web. Interpretations of what the Internet means to American Indians have ranged from assessments that enthusiastically embrace its liberatory promise to critiques that stress that it is antithetical to indigenous traditions. These debates have focused on four issues: traditional knowledge, traditional ways of knowing, community, and social power.

Proponents conceive of the Internet as a culturally neutral tool that affords American Indians a means with which to preserve their cultural heritage. It can be used to record the stories of elders and threatened languages for future generations. In contrast, critics see the World Wide Web as a technology that reflects Western biases and threatens traditional knowledge. Some fear that indigenous knowledge will be misunderstood and misused if it is made available online. Perhaps more troubling, the organization and exchange of information on the Internet conceives of knowledge as a resource or object; it threatens to reduce indigenous knowledge to sterile data that can be managed and controlled, taken out of context, repackaged, sold, and otherwise depleted of its sacredness.

Not only are the implications of the Internet for knowledge subject to debate, but there is much disagreement about how closely the Internet mirrors indigenous ways of knowing. Shoshone-Bannock journalist Mark Trahant and others see in the World Wide Web a close approximation of indigenous storytelling and oral traditions.[58] It is interactive and relational

The World Wide Web is not only an important means for educating Native American children, but it also serves to bring Native communities closer together. Shown here are students from the Wellpinit Elementary/High School on the Spokane Indian Reservation in Washington State.

like storytelling. Critics, in contrast, do not find tradition online, but think of its virtual worlds as the apex of Western ways of knowing that turn on objectification, detached observation, and consumption.

Much as they differ in the significance of knowing and knowledge online, proponents and critics of the Internet in Indian Country have distinct understandings of the relationship between the World Wide Web and the creation of community. One teacher in rural Canada encourages the use of computer-meditated technology, suggesting that it has positive benefits for nurturing community and student growth:

The rationale for using technology involving traditions and culture, and therefore the community, is to interest and

motivate students, bring the school and the community
closer together, create needed resources for the community,
and enhance understanding between students, staff, and
other people in the community.[59]

Mark Trahant also sees the Internet as a means to create community across time and space, a virtual community of inter-
connected individuals, affinities, and interests.

Critics counter that the World Wide Web presupposes and
values rootlessness and individualism, and consequently
undermines traditional notions of community as embodied,
interactive, and interdependent. Lakota scholar Craig Howe,
moreover, asserts that community demands—particularly for
indigenous peoples—a sense of place and a connection to the
land.[60] Consequently, he concludes:

> The Internet is an exceedingly deceptive technology whose
> power is immensely attractive to American Indians. But
> until its universalistic and individualistic foundation is
> restructured to incorporate spatial, social, spiritual, and
> experiential dimensions that particularize its application,
> cyberspace is no place for tribalism.[61]

Finally, the question of power and the Internet sharply
divides proponents and critics. Proponents conceive of the
World Wide Web as approximating the ideals of participatory
democracy, freeing knowledge from the constraints of the state,
while granting individuals, regardless of the circumstance, a
greater voice. For critics, the World Wide Web traces the contours of the real world, conforming to its stratified distribution
of opportunity, resources, wealth, and privilege. Consequently,
as noted earlier in this chapter, Native Americans have far less
access (and hence voice and opportunity). Worse, critics con-
tend, getting online draws Native Americans into a market
economy that undermines traditional values about community.

There is little middle ground in the debates over the
Internet in Indian Country. Whereas proponents hold that the

World Wide Web affords great possibility for indigenous communities (autonomy, preservation, and connection), critics assert that it threatens Native peoples (individualism, rootlessness, and market forces).

HOW TO ASSESS AN INTERNET SITE

It is important that users of the Internet be able to assess Web sites for their reliability. This is especially true when examining sites that make claims about American Indians, given the persistence of anti-Indian ideas in American culture, the possible harms of Internet technology for indigenous communities, and great diversity of sites on the Native nations of North America. Building on the work of Elaine M. Cubbins (*http://www.u.arizona.edu/~ecubbins/useful.html*), this section outlines a series of reminders and questions that can serve as useful guidelines when visiting Web sites on, by, for, or about American Indians.

To begin, it is important to remember that a Web page is a document, that like more traditional texts has a human author, and as such reflects the assumptions, position, agenda, and experience of the author. Web sites cannot be taken at face value, but should be questioned for what they say about Native Americans, from where they speak, what imagery and evidence they incorporate, their accuracy and authenticity, and their objectives and ends. Moreover, as the foregoing discussions of movies, mascots, and journalism remind us, even with the best intentions, stories and symbols can misuse and misrepresent indigenous cultures and histories. The same is true online. Finally, it is of fundamental importance to recall that Native Americans are real people from diverse backgrounds; they are human beings deserving of respect, which they often do not receive either online or in their everyday lives.

With this in mind, Cubbins encourages us to ask general questions about Web sites focusing on Native Americans, questions that one might ask of any Web site:

- How technologically sophisticated is the site? Does it preclude users who may lack the most current software?
- How current is the site? When was the last update?
- How easy is it to navigate?
- What links are included?
- What is the objective and position of the Web site?

More importantly, Cubbins rightly poses questions that relate to authority and content. Questions about authority encourage us to think about the author's capacity to speak about the topic (as an expert, participant, leader, or spokesperson) and the right to speak on behalf of a community or tribe:

- Who is the author? What can you learn about her/him? What is her/his purpose?
- Does the author identify as Indian? Does she/he specify tribal affiliation or enrollment?
- Is the Web site associated with or authorized by a Native nation or American Indian organization? Does the Web address include the suffix *nsn.us*?
- Is the Web site associated with an educational institution?
- Is the author an outsider? What are his/her motivations for building the site?
- Does the author use an insider or Native perspective? Does she/he have a right to do so?
- What credentials, experience, or authorization does the author highlight?

Answers to these questions tell us who is speaking, on what basis they can make claims, and should shape how one evaluates the information and arguments presented on the Web site. Questions about content prompt us to review the claims made at the Web site and their implications. Key points to consider when reading a Web site include:

- What is the purpose of the site? Is it selling something? Is it educational? Does it have a political objective (such as retiring mascots or ending treaty rights)?
- Who is the audience? Is it for tourists? Tribal members? Educators?
- What is the perspective? What evidence does it use to substantiate it?
- Does it employ stereotypes? Does it include caricatures and other disrespectful imagery? Does it present Native Americans in overly romanticized terms? What language does it employ?
- Is it accurate? Does it provide references to support its claims?
- Does it misuse traditional knowledge or spirituality?

Perhaps most importantly, Cubbins asks, does the Web site make "you feel uncomfortable?" If so, "ask knowledgeable people to evaluate it, notify tribes about sites to find out their opinions, and check reliable print and non-print sources (if possible) for verification."

In the end, as Elaine Cubbins underscores, "There is no one American Indian culture or people, so what is right for one tribe or nation is not automatically correct for another tribe or nation. Be careful what you believe to be true. Ask questions."[62] Hopefully, if the right questions are asked often enough, the World Wide Web can achieve its ideals of inclusion, openness, and electronic democracy.

THE FUTURE OF THE INTERNET AMONG NATIVE AMERICANS

For American Indians, the Internet has much in common with the other media reviewed in this book. Cyberspace, for all the talk of democracy and openness, is a technology controlled by corporations and driven by consumer demands, particularly those of its largest markets (educated, white men with disposable income). And because so many users of the Internet misunderstand indigenous peoples and the issues that impact them, this novel technology, like movies and news stories, can serve as a vehicle for the dissemination of false and hurtful ideas and the perpetuation of stereotypes. Moreover, Native Americans continue to have limited access to the World Wide Web as a result of economic impediments and social barriers. Consequently, as in television, film, and journalism, American Indians are not equal participants in the institutions, opportunities, and future of American society, nor are their perspectives fully audible to most Americans.

At the same time, the World Wide Web differs from other media, precisely because it hinges upon individual creativity and participation as much, if not more than, institutional control. Indeed, as a technology emerging in the wake of the cultural and political renaissance in Native America, which has fostered the growth of indigenous media, it is not surprising that the Internet also holds different prospects for American Indians. With a relatively small investment, individuals and organizations can tell broader, more diverse, and more distant audiences about themselves, their heritage, and the issues that matter to them. They can educate a broader public, engage in ongoing political struggles, and preserve practices, stories, and perspective that define who they are as a people. And, the World Wide Web has proven to be a useful economic tool for some communities and entrepreneurs, promoting tourism, tribal ventures, and small businesses. Significantly, for some critics in Indian Country, it is these features of the Internet, namely its emphasis on individualism and consumerism, that make it most dangerous to indigenous cultures.

In light of the history of the media and its treatment of Native Americans, the ongoing barriers to full participation online, and the dangers that the Internet may pose for indigenous communities, vigilance is crucial to the future of Indians in cyberspace. Authors and audiences of Web sites must become more critically literate, understanding how to assess and analyze Web sites containing Indian content. In part, this means that existing stereotypes are challenged and that guidelines like those discussed in this chapter become common knowledge. Policy makers and community, education, and business leaders must work to find ways to increase Native participation online without hurting individuals, traditions, or communities. On the one hand, more initiatives like the Bill and Melinda Gates Foundation's Native American Access to Technology Program need to be undertaken; and, on the other hand, it means that indigenous perspectives and concerns must become more central to the development and use of new technologies as the foundation for education, community, and democracy. In short, the future of the World Wide Web, much the same as other media that represent Native Americans, depends on the sensitivity and attentiveness with which questions about diversity, inclusion, equality, and possibility are addressed in the present.

1829   *Cherokee Phoenix and Indian Advocate* founded.

1893   Buffalo Bill's Wild West show is the hit attraction at the Columbian Exhibition Midway.

1910   James Young Deer directs *White Fawn's Devotion.*

1911   James Young Deer named head of Pathe's West Coast Studios.

1928   Edwin Carewe directs *Ramona.*

1961   American Indian Conference held in Chicago.

1962   Institute of American Indian Arts (IAIA) founded in Santa Fe, New Mexico.

1968   The National Congress of American Indians challenges media stereotypes.

1969   Indians of All Nations occupy Alcatraz Island in California.

1971   Marquette University drops its "Willie Wampum" mascot, becoming the Golden Eagles in 1994; American Indian Press Association founded.

1972   Stanford University changes its mascot from the Indians to Cardinal.

1977   Native American Public Broadcasting Consortium created.

1988   Indian Gaming Regulatory Act passed.

1990   *Dances with Wolves* makes its debut.

1996   Miami University of Ohio changes its mascot from the Redskins to the Redhawks.

1997   The Board of Education for the Los Angeles, California, consolidated school district votes to eliminate Indian-related mascots.

1998   *Smoke Signals* is released.

2001   The U.S. Commission on Civil Rights issues a position paper against American Indian mascots.

2002   *The Business of Fancydancing, Fast Runner,* and *Skins* all released.

Chapter 1:
Introduction and Overview

1 E.M. Swift, "On the Wild Side," *Sports Illustrated*, August 18, 2003, 54.

2 Ibid.

3 Ibid.

Chapter 2:
Films and Television

4 Ralph Friar and Natasha Friar, *The Only Good Indian: The Hollywood Gospel* (New York: Drama Book Specialists, 1972), 96.

5 Ibid.

6 Ward Churchill, "American Indians in Film: Thematic Contours of Cinematic Colonization," in *Reversing the Lens: Ethnicity, Race, Gender, and Sexuality through Film*, Jun Xing and Lane Ryo Hirabayashi, eds. (Boulder, Colo.: University of Press of Colorado, 2003), 43.

7 Jacquelyn Kilpatrick, *Celluloid Indians: Native Americans and Film* (Lincoln, Nebr.: University of Nebraska Press, 1999).

8 Beverly R. Singer, *Wiping the War Paint off the Lens: Native American Film and Video* (Minneapolis, Minn.: University of Minnesota Press, 2001), 44.

9 Kilpatrick, *Celluloid Indians*, 151.

10 Rob Schmidt, "Voodoo Villain Hurts *The Missing*," December 11, 2003: *http://www.bluecorncomics.com/missing.htm* (accessed January 14, 2004).

Chapter 3:
Journalistic Coverage

11 Native American Journalists Association, "NAJA Reacts to the Outkast Performance": *http://www.naja.com/outkast_021604.html*.

12 James E. Murphy and Sharon M. Murphy, *Let My People Know: American Indian Journalism, 1828–1978* (Norman, Okla.: University of Oklahoma Press, 1981), 5.

13 Ibid.

14 John M. Coward, *The Newspaper Indian: Native American Identity in the Press, 1820–1890* (Urbana, Ill.: University of Illinois Press, 1999), 73.

15 Ibid., 233.

16 Mary Ann Weston, *Native Americans in the News: Images of Indians in the Twentieth Century Press* (Westport, Conn.: Greenwood Press, 1996), 78.

17 Ibid., 24.

18 Ibid., 25.

19 Ibid., 87.

20 Ibid., 93

21 Ibid., 105.

22 Ibid., 106.

23 Ibid.

24 Ibid.

25 Joseph Allen, "The More Things Really Don't Change," in *The American Indian and the Media*, 2nd ed, edited by Mark Anthony Rolo (St. Paul, Minn.: National Conference for Community and Justice, 2000), 20–22.

26 Kara Briggs, Tom Arviso, Dennis McAuliffe, and Lori Edmo-Suppah, "The Reading Red Report. Native Americans in the News: A 2002 Report and Content Analysis on Coverage by the Largest Newspapers in the United States" (Native American Journalists Association and News Watch, 2002).

27 Ibid., VIII–IX.

28 Ibid., XII.

29 Ibid., XIX.

30 Ibid., VIII.

31 Jay Rosenstein, "In Whose Honor?, Mascots, and the Media," in *Team Spirits: The Native American Mascots Controversy*, edited by C. Richard King and Charles F. Springwood (Lincoln, Nebr.: University of Nebraska Press, 2001).

32 Robert Kaplan, "It's Time to Remember the Lessons of the Indian Wars," *Wall Street Journal*, September 21, 2004.

Chapter 4:
Mascots

33 Without Rezervations, *Are You Ready for W.O.R?* (Phoenix, Ariz.: Canyon Records, 1994).

34 Robert F. Berkhofer, *The White Man's Indian: Images of the American Indian from Columbus to Present* (New York: Vintage/Random House, 1978).

35 Webster Schuyler, Patricia Loudbear, David Corn, and Bernard Vigue. "Four MU Indian Students Describe Willie Wampum as Racist Symbol," *The Marquette Tribune*, February 17, 1971. See also C. Richard King, "Uneasy

Indians: Creating and Contesting Native American Mascots at Marquette University," in *Team Spirits: The Native American Mascots Controversy*, edited by C. Richard King and Charles F. Springwood (Lincoln, Nebr.: University of Nebraska Press, 2001), 281–303.

36 "Southeastern Oklahoma State Has Discussed Future of Mascot," *Daily Ardmoreite*, May 7, 2001, 7.

37 Dale W. Lick, "Seminoles—Heroic Symbol at Florida State": *http://seminoles.fansonly.com/trads/fsu-trads-seminoles.html* (accessed May 23, 2000).

38 For a good example see Ward Churchill, "Let's Spread the Fun Around," in *Indians Are Us? Culture and Genocide in Native North America* (Monroe, Maine: Common Courage Press, 1994), 65–72. C. Richard King offers a useful analysis of such metaphors in the mascot debate in his recent essay: "Borrowing Power: Racial Metaphors and Pseudo-Indian Mascots," in *CR: The New Centennial Review* 4 (2004): 189–209.

39 Jesse Villalobos, personal communication, August, 15, 2001.

40 Letter from the University of Illinois Department of Anthropology, February 17, 1998: *http://www2.uiuc.edu/unit/senate/eq9704_b.html* (accessed March 1, 2005).

Chapter 5:
Indigenous Media

41 S. Elizabeth Bird, *The Audience in Everyday Life: Living in a Media World* (New York: Routledge, 2003).

42 Michael C. Keith, *Signals in the Air: Native Broadcasting in America* (Westport, Conn.: Praeger, 1995); Mark N. Trahant, *Pictures of Our Nobler Selves: A History of Native American Contributions to News Media* (Nashville, Tenn.: Free Forum First Amendment Center, 1995).

43 Ibid., 21.

44 Murphy and Murphy, *Let My People Know: American Indian Journalism, 1828–1978*, 33–34.

45 Ibid., 37.

46 Ibid.

47 John M. Coward, "Explaining the Little Bighorn," in *Outsiders in the 19th Century Press*, edited by Frankie Hutton and Barbara Strauss Reed (Bowling Green, Ohio: Bowling Green State University Popular Press, 1995).

48 Ibid.

49 Beverly R. Singer, *Wiping the War Paint off the Lens: Native American Film and Video* (Minneapolis, Minn.: University of Minnesota Press, 2001), 24.

50 Ibid., 39–40.

51 Ibid., 96.

52 Ibid., 62.

53 Ibid., xiii.

Chapter 6:
The Internet and the Future of Native Americans in the Media

54 Andrew C. Gordon, Jessica Dorr, and Margaret Gordon, "Native American Technology Access: The Gates Foundation in Four Corners," *The Electronic Library* 21 (2003): 428.

55 Native American Technology Access, 429.

56 Lisa Mitten. "Indians on the Internet—Selected Native American Web Sites." *The Electronic Library* 21 (2003): 443–449.

57 Ellen L. Arnold and Darcy C. Plymire, "The Cherokee Indians and the Internet," in *Web Studies: Rewriting Media Studies for a Digital Age*, edited by David Gauntlett (New York: Oxford University Press, 2000). See also Cokie Gaston Anderson, "American Indian Tribal Web sites: A Review and Comparison," *The Electronic Library* 21 (2003): 450–355.

58 Mark N. Trahant, "The Power of Stories: Native Words and Images on the Internet,"

Native Americas 13 (1996): 15–21.

59   C.A. Bowers, Miguel Vasquez, and Mary
     Roaf, "Native People and the Challenge of
     Computers: Reservation Schools,
     Individualism, and Consumerism," in
     American Indian Quarterly 24 (2000): 183.

60   Craig Howe, "Cyberspace Is No Place for

Tribalism," *Wicazo-Sa Review* 13 (1999).

61   Ibid.

62   Elaine Cubbins, "Techniques for Evaluating
     American Indian Web Sites":
     *http://www.u.arizona.edu/~ecubbins/
     useful.html.*

Bibliography

"American Indian Sport Team Mascot Archive": *http://www.aistm.org/1ind-expage.htm.*

Anderson, Cokie Gaston. "American Indian Tribal Web Sites: A Review and Comparison." *The Electronic Library* 21 (2003), 450–355.

Arnold, Ellen L., and Darcy C. Plymire. "The Cherokee Indians and the Internet." In *Web Studies: Rewriting Media Studies for a Digital Age,* edited by David Gauntlett. New York: Oxford University Press, 2000.

Berkhofer, Robert F. *The White Man's Indian: Images of the American Indian from Columbus to Present:* New York: Vintage/Random House, 1978.

Bird, S. Elizabeth, ed. *Dressing in Feathers: The Construction of the Indian in American Popular Culture.* Boulder, Colo.: Westview, 1996.

Bowers, C.A., Miguel Vasquez, and Mary Roaf. "Native People and the Challenge of Computers: Reservation Schools, Individualism, and Consumerism." *American Indian Quarterly* 24 (2000): 182–199.

Briggs, Kara, Tom Arviso, Dennis McAuliffe, and Lori Edmo-Suppah. "The Reading Red Report. Native Americans in the News: A 2002 Report and Content Analysis on Coverage by the Largest Newspapers in the United States." Native American Journalists Association and News Watch, 2002.

Churchill, Ward. "Let's Spread the Fun Around." In *Indians Are Us? Culture and Genocide in Native North America,* 65–72. Monroe, Maine: Common Courage Press, 1994.

Coward, John M. *The Newspaper Indian: Native American Identity in the Press, 1820–1890.* Urbana, Ill.: University of Illinois Press, 1999.

Davis, Laurel R. "The Problems with Native American Mascots." *Multicultural Education* 9 (2002): 11–14.

Friar, Ralph, and Natasha Friar. *The Only Good Indian: The Hollywood Gospel.* New York: Drama Book Specialists, 1972.

Gordon, Andrew C., Jessica Dorr, and Margaret Gordon. "Native American Technology Access: The Gates Foundation in Four Corners." *The Electronic Library,* 21, 5 (2003).

Howe, Craig. "Cyberspace Is No Place for Tribalism." *Wicazo-Sa Review* 13, 2 (1999).

Keith, Michael C. *Signals in the Air: Native Broadcasting in America.* Westport, Conn.: Praeger, 1995.

Kilpatrick, Jacquelyn. *Celluloid Indians: Native Americans and Film.* Lincoln, Nebr.: University of Nebraska Press, 1999.

King, C. Richard. *The Native American Mascots Controversy: A Sourcebook* (forthcoming). Lanham, Md.: Scarecrow Books.

_____, and Charles F. Springwood, eds. *Team Spirits: The Native American Mascots Controversy.* Lincoln, Nebr.: University of Nebraska, 2001.

Mitten, Lisa. "Indians on the Internet—Selected Native American Web Sites." *The Electronic Library* 21(5) 2003: 443–449.

Moses, L.G. *Wild West Shows and the Images of American Indians, 1883–1933.* Albuquerque, N.M.: University of New Mexico Press, 1996.

Murphy, James E., and Sharon M. Murphy. *Let My People Know: American Indian Journalism, 1828–1978.* Norman, Okla.: University of Oklahoma Press, 1981.

Pewewardy, Cornell D. "Native American Mascots and Imagery: The Struggle of Unlearning Indian Stereotypes." *Journal of Navaho Education* 9 (1991): 19–23.

Singer, Beverly R. *Wiping the War Paint off the Lens: Native American Film and Video.* Minneapolis, Minn.: University of Minnesota Press, 2001.

Spindel, Carol. *Dancing at Halftime: Sports and the Controversy over American Indian Mascots.* New York: New York University Press, 2000.

Staurowsky, Ellen J. "American Indian Imagery and the Miseducation of America." *Quest,* 51 (1999): 382–392.

Steadman, Raymond William. *Shadows of the Indian: Stereotypes in American Culture.* Norman, Okla.: University of Oklahoma Press, 1982.

Trahant, Mark N. *Pictures of Our Nobler Selves: A History of Native American Contributions to News Media.* Nashville, Tenn.: Free Forum First Amendment Center, 1995.

———. "The Power of Stories: Native Words and Images on the Internet." *Native Americas* 13 (1996): 15–21.

Weston, Mary Ann. *Native Americans in the News: Images of Indians in the Twentieth Century Press.* Westport, Conn.: Greenwood Press, 1996.

Further Reading

Books

Berkhofer, Robert F. *The White Man's Indian: Images of the American Indian from Columbus to Present.* New York: Vintage/Random House, 1978.

Briggs, Kara, Tom Arviso, Dennis McAuliffe, and Lori Edmo-Suppah. "The Reading Red Report. Native Americans in the News: A 2002 Report and Content Analysis on Coverage by the Largest Newspapers in the United States." Native American Journalists Association and News Watch, 2002.

Deloria, Philip. *Indians in Unexpected Places.* Lawrence, Kans.: University Press of Kansas, 2004.

King, C. Richard, and Charles F. Springwood, eds. *Team Spirits: The Native American Mascots Controversy.* Lincoln, Nebr.: University of Nebraska Press, 2001.

Rolo, Mark Anthony, ed. *The American Indian and the Media*, 2nd edition. St. Paul, Minn.: National Conference for Community and Justice.

Singer, Beverly R. *Wiping the War Paint off the Lens: Native American Film and Video.* Minneapolis, Minn.: University of Minnesota Press, 2001.

Steadman, Raymond William. *Shadows of the Indian: Stereotypes in American Culture.* Norman, Okla.: University of Oklahoma Press, 1982.

Trahant, Mark N. *Pictures of Our Nobler Selves: A History of Native American Contributions to News Media.* Nashville, Tenn.: Free Forum First Amendment Center, 1995.

Websites

National Coalition on Sports and the Media
http://www.aics.org/NCRSM/index.htm

American Indian Sports Team Mascots
http://www.aistm.org/1indexpage.htm

Native American Sports Council
http://nascsports.org

Native American Journalists Association
http://www.naja.com/

Films and Videos about Native Peoples
http://www.nativevideos.com/

Films and Videos on Native Topics
http://www.visionmaker.org/

Index

Afghanistan, 13, 50–51
Alexie, Sherman, 27, 83, 85–86
Allen, Joseph
  on American journalism and the
    American Indian, 46
American (newspaper), 73
American Anthropology Association,
  59
American Film Institute, 81
American Indian Conference (1961),
  41
American Indian Film Institute, 82
American Indian Higher Education
  Consortium, 81, 92–93
American Indian Movement (AIM),
  42, 59
American Indian Press, 75, 76
  and commitment to educate, 77–78
  contributions of, 73–74
  and lack of First Amendment protec-
    tions, 79–80
American Indian Trust Fund, 47
Apple Computer, 89
Apted, Michael, 84
Arizonian (newspaper), 37
Arkansian (newspaper), 73
Arnold, Ellen L., 94
Arvison, Tom, 46–47
A'tome (newspaper), 77

Backbone of the World: The Blackfeet
  (film), 81
Battle at Elderbrush Gulch (film),
  17–18, 22
Battle of Little Bighorn, 36, 78
Beebe, Tanna, 74
Berkhofer, Robert, 53
Bigcrane, Roy, 81
Bird, Elizabeth, 71
Bird, Gloria, 81
Black Robe (film), 20, 23
Boston Tea Party, 56
Boudinot, Elias C., 73, 75–76
Boudinot, William P., 79
Bowman, Arlene, 85–86

Briggs, Kara, 46–47
Broken Arrow (film), 18, 22, 26
Buffalo Bill Cody, 14, 15, 16–17
Burdeau, George, 81, 85
Bureau of Indian Affairs (BIA), 47, 80
Bursum Bill, 39
Bursum, Holm Olaf, 39
Bush, W. Stephen, 10
Bushyhead, Edward, 73–74
Business of Fancy Dancing, The (film),
  85–86
Bustamante, Cruz, 48

Camp Grant Massacre, 36–37
Cannes Film Festival, 86
Carewe, Edwin, 15–16
Char-Koosta (newspaper), 74–75
Cherokee Advocate (newspaper), 76, 78,
  79
Cherokee Nation, 76, 93–94
Cherokee Phoenix (newspaper), 6,
  75–76
Cheyenne Autumn (film), 18
Chicago Sun-Times 46–47
Churchill, Ward, 12–14
Circle, The (newspaper), 46
Cleveland Indians, 7, 57
Collier's, 40
Costner, Kevin, 5
Cubbins, Elaine M., 99–100, 101
Current Events (Adahooniligii),
  newsletter, 75
Custer's Last Stand, 36, 78
Cyberspace, 8

Dance for the New Generation (film),
  85
Dances with Wolves (film), 5, 20, 22, 23,
  24, 25, 26, 44
Davis, Gray, 48
Deer, James Young, 15–16
Died with Their Boots On, They (film),
  18
Dix, Richard, 17

Index

Dr. Quinn Medicine Woman, (T.V. show), 20

Eaglestaff, Robert, 27
Early Show, 45
Eddleman, Myrta, 73–74
Edison, Thomas, 14
Elk, Molly Spotted, 15–16
Ernie Peppion: The Human Touch (biography), Macy, 81
Euro-American, 4, 5, 54, 55, 71, 72
Everything Has a Spirit (film), 85
Eyre, Chris, 27, 83, 86

Fast Runner (film), 86
Film, 10
  on false representations of American Indians, 11
  featuring Native American themes, 12
First Blood (film), 19
Florida State University, 62
Foundation's Native American Access to Technology Program, 103
Frito Bandito, 58, 64

Gates, Bill, 103
Gates, Melinda, 103
Geiogamah, Hanay, 85
George Horse Capture, 84
Ghost Dance, 36
Grammy Awards (2004), 31, 95, 96
Griffith, D.W., 17–18

Hamilton, Ava, 85
Harjo, Joy, 81
Harjo, Suzan Shown, 53
Harper's Monthly, 35
Harrington, John P., 75
Harrington-LaFarge alphabet, 75
Her Giveaway (film), 85
Hollywood Images, 28–29
Hollywood Indian, 11, 20, 21, 29, 32, 50, 71
Houston Chronicle (newspaper), 46–47

Howe, Craig, 98
Hunkpapa Sioux, 15

Ickes, Harold L., 40
Illiniwek (Chief), mascot, 55, 57, 61, 67–68, 69, 91
Imagining Indians (film), 84
Indian Country Today (newspaper), 74
Indian Gaming, 48
Indian Gaming Regulatory Act, 48
Indians Have a Name for Hitler (article), 40
Indian Wars, The (film), 17
Institute of American Indian Arts (IAIA), 80
Intelligencer (newspaper), 76–77
Internet, 92–99
  on assessing a site, 99–101
  on barriers for Native Americans, 90–91
  the future of for Native Americans, 101–103
Inuk, 1
Iraq, 13, 50–51

Johnson, Glen, 61

Kalem and Lubin (film company), 16
Kaplan, Steven, 50–51
Kauffman, Hattie (Nez Perce), 44, 74
  and news correspondent, 45
KDFN (Wyoming), 74

Ladies Home Journal, 39
LaFarge, Oliver, 75
Language, 22–23
Larry Littlebird, 84
Last of the Dogmen (film), 20
Last of the Mohicans (film), 20–21, 25, 26
Lick, Dale W., 62–63
Lighting the 7th Fire (film), 85
Little Big Man (film), 19, 25–26
Lone Ranger (T.V. show), 18
Los Angeles Times, 46–47

Lucas, Phil, 85
Lynch, Jessica, 13

Macy, Terry, 81
Major League Baseball, 7
Man Called Horse, A (film), 19
Marquette University, 57–58, 59, 61
Masayesva, Victor, 84
Mascot (song), 52
Mascots, 52
  on changes, 59–60
  controversies of, 47, 57–61
  in defense of, 62–64
  and educational institutions, 66–69
  history of, 55–57
  and imagery in athletics, 53–55,
    58–59, 66–67
  opposition of, 64–65
  on public opinion polls, 54
  significance of, 65–66
  on thriving, 69–70
Massacre (film), 17–18
Mass media, 3, 5, 8
  and Native Americans, 6
Maynor, Malinda, 85–86
Merritt, Wesley, 35
Miles, Elaine, 24
Milo Yellow Hair, 81
Mitten, Lisa, 92
Modern Language Association, 59
Modern Western, 18
Montana State University, 81
Morning Star Institute, 53
Moving Picture Absurdities (essay), 10
Moving Picture World, 10–11
Murrow, Edward R., 50
Muskogee Daily Times (newspaper),
    73–74

Nashville Predators, 1, 3
National Collegiate Athletic
    Association (NCAA), 68
National Congress of American
    Indians, 59
National Education Association, 59

National Hockey League, 1, 3, 6
National Museum of the American
    Indian (New York), 82
Native American Cinematic Themes,
    84–87
Native American Film, 80–88
Native American Journalists
    Association (NAJA), 32, 46, 77, 79
Native American News (newspaper), 74
Native American Public Broadcasting
    Consortium (1977), 80
Native American Public
    Telecommunications (NAPT),
    1995, 80–81, 93
Native Americans, 2, 9, 71
  and challenging media images, 6
  on correcting false images of them, 7
  and protesting cinematic representa-
    tion, 10–11
  stereotyping of, 4–5, 13
Native American Web sites, 92–96
Native Nevadan (newspaper), 74
Native Voices Public Television
    Workshop, 81
Navajo Reservation, 90
Navajo Talking Picture (film), 85–86
Navajo Times (newspaper), 74, 75
Navarre, Peter, 73–74
Newspaper Indian, 33–38, 43, 51
News Watch, 46
Newsweek, 41
New York Daily News, 46–47
New York Times, 39, 42, 46–47
New York University, 81–82
Nineteenth-Century Journalism, 34–38
North America, 8–9
Northern Exposure (T.V. show), 20, 23,
    24, 71
Northwest Passage (film), 18

*On and Off the Reservation with
    Charlie Hill* (film), 84
Online Activism, 95
Operation Mayflower, 13
Osawa, Sandra, 84, 85

Index

Osceola (Chief), 55
Outkast (hip-hop group), 31, 32, 95, 96

Pathe Company West Coast Studio, 16
Piestewa, Lori Ann, 13
Place of Falling Waters, The (documentary), Bigcrane, 81
Plymire, Darcy C., 94
Pocahontas (film), 20–21, 22, 24, 27, 44
Polatkin, Seymour, 86
Portland Oregonian (newspaper), 60
Powwow Highway (film), 19–20, 23, 27
Prospector and the Indian, The (film), 16
Pueblo Indians, 39
Pueblo Legend (film), 17–18
Pyle, Ernie, 40

Ramona (film), 15–16
Rankin Inlet, 2, 4
Rather Be Powwowing, I'd (film), 84
"Reading Red Report, The" (Briggs/Arvison/McAuliffe/ Edmo-Suppah), 46–47
findings of, 47, 49–50
Real Indians (film), 85–86
Red Eagle, The Lawyer (film), 16
Red Wing's Gratitude (film), 16
Reed, Ora Eddleman, (Sunshine Lady), 74
Reyna, Diane, 85
Ridge, John Rollin, 73
Robinson, Rose W., 74
Rogers' Rangers, 18
Ross, W.P., 76
Rossville Reporter (newspaper), 73–74

Sacramento Bee (newspaper), 73
San Diego State University, 60, 61
San Diego Union (newspaper), 73–74
Scouts to the Rescue (film), 23
Seals, Huron David, 27
Selden, Charles A., 39
Silent Enemy (film), 16
Silent film era, 14, 16–17, 18, 23–24

Singer, Beverly, 84, 87
Sioux Ghost Dance and Indian War Council, 14
Sitting Bull, 15
Skins (film), 83, 85, 86
Smith, Mona, 85
Smithsonian Institution, 75
Smoke Signals (film), 27, 83, 84, 86
Soldier Blue (film), 19
Southeastern Oklahoma State University, 61
Spirit of Crazy Horse, In the (documentary), Milo Yellow Hair, 81
Spokane Indian Reservation, 97
Sports Illustrated, 1, 5, 6
and stereotyping, 4
Stagecoach (film), 18, 19
St. Cyr, Lillian, 16
Stereotype, 5–6, 8, 29, 43, 48
definition of, 3
and the media, 5
and racial, 4
Strickland, Rennard, 21–22
Strom, Karen, 92
Surviving Columbus: The Story of the Pueblo People (film), 85

Talk Leaf (newspaper), 74
Tell Them Willie Boy Is Here (film), 19
Three Indian Campaigns (Merritt), 35
Thunderheart (film), 20, 84
Tootoo, Jordin, 1, 6
and how he is portrayed, 2
a player for the Nashville Predators, 3
Trademark Trial and Appeal Board, 59–60
Trahant, Mark N., (Shoshone-Bannock), 44
and the internet, 96, 97
Tribal casinos, 47
benefits of, 48
misconceptions of, 48
Twentieth-century journalism, 38–43
Twin Peaks (T.V. show), 20, 23

Index

Two Rivers Native American Film and Video Festival (1991), 82
Typecasting, 13

Umatilla Reservation, 24
Unitarian Universalist Association of Congregations, 59
United Church of Christ, 59
United Methodist Church, 59
USA Today, 46–47
United States Civil Rights Commission, 59
University of Illinois, 61, 67–68
University of North Dakota, 69

Vanishing American, The (film), 17, 18, 25–26
Visionmaker Video (production company), 81

Wahoo (Chief), 64, 91
  as mascot, 7, 55
Waite, Charles, 73

Wall Street Journal, 46–47, 50–51
Warfare
  on misrepresentation of American Indians, 13
War Party (film), 20, 23
Washington Post, 46–47
Weapons systems, 13
Weekly Arizona, 36–37
Wellpinit School, 97
White Fawn's Devotion (film), 15–16
Wild West shows, 5, 15
  on the American Indian, 11
  and impact on American culture, 12, 16
Windtalkers (film), 20
Wipe the War Paint off the Lens (Singer), 84
Without Rezervations, 52
Worth, Sol, 80
Wounded Knee Massacre, 17, 42

Yakama Nation Review (newspaper), 74
Yaqui Girl (film), 15–16

page:

C. Richard King, Ph.D., is Associate Professor of Comparative Ethnic Studies at Washington State University. King has published several books on the social experiences of Native Americans, including *Team Spirits: The Native American Mascots Controversy* and *Native Americans in Sports*. His articles have appeared in such publications as *American Indian Culture and Research Journal* and the *Journal of Sport and Social Issues*.

Paul C. Rosier received his Ph.D. in American History from the University of Rochester, with a specialty in Native American History. His first book, *Rebirth of the Blackfeet Nation, 1912–1954*, was published by the University of Nebraska Press in 2001. In November 2003, Greenwood Press published *Native American Issues* as part of its Contemporary American Ethnic Issues series. Dr. Rosier has also published articles on Native American topics in the *American Indian Culture and Research Journal*, and the *Journal of American Ethnic History*. In addition, he was coeditor of *The American Years: A Chronology of United States History*. He is Assistant Professor of History at Villanova University, where he also serves as a faculty advisor to the Villanova Native American Student Association.

Walter Echo-Hawk is a member of the Pawnee tribe. He is a staff attorney for the Native American Rights Fund (*www.narf.org*) and a Justice on the Supreme Court of the Pawnee Nation (*www.pawneenation.org/court*). He has handled cases and legislation affecting Native American rights in areas such as religious freedom, education, water rights, fishing rights, grave protection, and tribal repatriation of Native dead.